No

I Andrew Baker, hereby assert and give notice of my right
under section 77 of the copyright, designs and patents Act 1988
to be identified as the author of the forgoing work.

Andrew Baker

Typesetting by
Well Thought Out Publication
and
Fairmaiden Reprographics

Published 2013 by
A Well Thought Out Publication.

First published by Direct-Pod; part of the Lonsdale Direct
Solutions Group Ltd.
Contact Agent at; www.yarnspinnersweb.com
ISBN: 978-0-9529984-5-7

A Souvenir History Of Kingston Prison

Introducing Stories and Poems by prisoners.

Andrew Baker

Dedicated to; the victims of crime and the innocent
prisoners still incarcerated.

Acknowledgements

I doubt if any one would like to serve time in any prison, however, over 90,000 men, women, and children have already decided to take up crime as a way of life and found themselves imprisoned in penal establishments such as HM Prison Kingston depicted in the following pages.

In many cases during my research I have based my findings on detailed descriptions presented to me by various Town and County records offices, and indeed those of the Governors at the prisons.

The sources are so numerous that an attempt to list them all would cover several pages. Kingston prison I have seen at first hand, but I could not spend too much time in it, so I thank the researchers who have helped make this work possible, and I am personally indebted to the Governor of Her Majesty's Prison Kingston.

In some instances I have used verbal material from serving prisoners, and indeed prison officers. Their sharp and knowledgeable memories revealed many aspects of prison life, and on occasions unveiled some details that I would otherwise have missed and that had never been noted before. So I am grateful to them. I am also indebted to the Kingston Magazine; KM for allowing me to reproduce stories and poems written by prisoners.

I am also grateful to Portsmouth City Library, The Portsmouth Papers, The Portsmouth News and Officers that served in Kingston before its closure.

Contents Page

Who said What!

'The risk, under the conditions as they exist in this country, of the capital penalty being executed on anyone who was not in fact guilty of the crime of which he has been convicted is so small, and indeed so infinitesimal that consideration can be dismissed.'
A former Home Secretary, 14th April 1948.

'He might have not have been innocent of the crime of which he was accused, but if he was charged with it, it was because he belonged to the classes amongst whom they looked for crime.'
Rt. Hon. Sir Robert Lowe, former Home Secretary, 25 July, 1879.

'It is a capital mistake to theorize before one has data. Insensibly one begins to trust facts to suit facts.'
Sir Arthur Conan Doyle; (A Scandal in Bohemia).

'Consider, Sir, what is the purpose of courts of justice? It is that every man shall have his case fairly tried by men appointed to try causes.'
Doctor Johnson.

Glossary of Prison Slang

Glossary of prison slang and language The following words do not necessarily appear in the foregoing text; they are included to give the reader an idea of the language used in prisons.

Judas hole;	Spyhole; /observation hole/aperture in cell door.
Screw;	Prison Officer.
Snout;	Tobacco
Nonce;	Sex offender.
Bacon;	Sex offender.
V.P.;	Vulnerable prisoner.
V.P.U;	Vulnerable Prisoners Unit.
Skins;	Cigarette papers.
Grass;	Informer.
Cat 'A'	High security risk prisoner.
Red Band;	Trustee.
Blue Band;	Trustee, (with more trust).
Green band;	Trustee, (with yet more trust).
Peter;	Cell, (as in safe).
Diesel;	Tea.
Powder;	Quantity of Cocaine.
Spliff;	Hand rolled cigarette, containing Marijuana
Puff;	Quantity of Marijuana.
Pipe;	Object, (usually a biro pen casing), used to smoke Marijuana.
No. 1;	Number One Governor.
A.G.;	Assistant Governor.
Dep;	Deputy Governor.
Spoon;	Cell key.
Lag;	Recidivist, or prisoner who has served 2 years or more.
Lagging;	Prison sentence of 2 years.
Seg.;	Segregation unit.

Block;	Segregation unit.
Choky;	Bread and water, (no longer in use, but now known as the segregation unit).
Vet;	Prison doctor.
Quack;	Prison doctor.
Wings;	Accommodation blocks.
Centre;	Main controlling point of the prison.
Y.P.;	Young Prisoner.
On stage;	Extra privileges earned, (no longer officially in use).
Basic;	Lowest behavioural category.
Standard;	Intermediate behavioural category.
Enhanced;	Highest behavioural category.
Tally;	Cell indicator.
Flag;	Cell indicator.
Slop out;	Disposing waste from previous night into disposal latrine in recess. (still happens in some prisons).
Hooch;	Illegal brew of alcohol.
The yard;	Exercise area.
Doing a runner;	Escaping from custody.
Burglars;	Security officers.
Spin;	Cell search.
Special;	Cell search, (when grassed up).
Listener;	Inmate affiliated to the Samaritans
Association;	Recreation period.
On the door;	Kicking and banging cell door (usually in protest).
Mug shot;	Photograph taken for record, (head and shoulders)
Landings;	Accommodation floor level.
Walkways;	Accommodation floor level gangways.
Chief;	Most senior officer, (no longer in use).
Tooled up;	Carrying a weapon.
Wired up;	Wiring of radio into the electric light circuit.
Nicked;	Placed on report.
Porridge;	Doing time, (sentence).
Visits;	Social visits from friends/relatives.
Brief;	Solicitor.
D.L.P.;	Discretionary Lifers Panel.

Board;	Interview for parole, etc.
V.C.;	Visiting Committee, (not used now).
Barricading up;	Using cell furniture to block up door.
Smashing up;	Destroying all cell fixture and fittings.
Cut up;	Using knife or razor blade to inflict wound to prisoner's face.
Blade;	Knife, (made in prison workshop).
Topped himself;	Committed suicide.
Strip search;	Body search, (usually after social visits).
Recess;	Area set aside within accommodation blocks to dispose of waste.
Stitched up;	Falsely accused by prison officer.
Con;	Prisoner/short for convict.
Banged up;	Locked up in cell.
Lock down;	Every prisoner in the prison locked up.
Grapevine;	Prisoner's underground communication line.
Kangaroo;	Screw.
Bag;	Small quantity of Heroin.
Volumetric Control;	Two large boxes to contain a prisoners belongings and that is all they are allowed.

Introduction

These Cursed Places...

A stout forbidding door creaks on its rusty iron hinges and crashes open. A long dark and dreary corridor stretches into the distance, cold and dimly lit by foul smelling oil lamps. Gruesome dancing shadows play mind games in these places full of sad, haunting memories and unspeakable secrets.

'A Souvenir History of Kingston Prison ' is not for the faint-hearted, it will give the reader an insight into the world of prisoners' their habitat and life-styles from before Victorian times prior to its closure on April 1st 2013.

What induced prisoners to write such beautiful poems and imaginative short stories. What secrets did these places hold? The harsh reality of a prisoner's world comes alive as 'A Souvenir History of Kingston Prison' reveals the secrets of these stark and sombre cells. The long walks to the gallows (even though prisoners awaiting execution were taken to Winchester to meet their maker). The floggings, murders, riots... and more.

A Souvenir History Of Kingston Prison

Portsmouth's first gaol was built in the High Street according to the Corporation's records of 1569 and was known as the Whitehouse. At first sight this building gave the appearance of an ordinary dwelling; for it was sandwiched between the vicarage and the Crown Inn. The premises were sold for £1,000 in 1805 and a hotel built on the site. Nevertheless before the gaol was put on the market there were several scandalous reports concerning discipline and drunkenness amongst prisoners and staff.

In 1802, James Neild, a writer, referred to it as 'This wretched gaol.' A gaol where even debtors found it extremely difficult to pay off their debts.

The following Letter was written by a debtor in the Whitehouse to the Mayor and is dated May 3, 1705.

'I hope you will excuse my boldness as this comes to acquaint your worships that I am detained here as a prisoner of Mr. Martin, of this town for debt and for not producing my duplicate, (receipt), which I normally carried about with me. I was discharged almost twelve month ago as a partisan paid off my debt. I humbly pray your worship to send for Mr. Foster, so that I may come before your worships and so wait according to my acts. I remain your Worships' most humble and obedient servant.

Jetro Chapman

Jetro Chapman added the following text at the end of his letter to the Mayor. 'It is my duty by my duplicate to apply to your worship to release me; for without the necessary papers I cannot see why Mr Martin can detain me, or show any cause of action against me.'

Little is known about where prisoners were held after the Whitehouse was closed. It is presumed they were incarcerated in the hulks, which littered both Portsmouth and Langstone harbours and there they stayed until the Borough Gaol was erected in Penny Street; near where the old barracks were, and now the site of Portsmouth Grammar School, (1808).

Here are some extracts from the Visiting Justices' Book at the Borough Gaol, 1848-49.1849;

March 13. In consequences of the convicted felons in No 2 and No 4, having expressed through the Governor of the Gaol, a wish to see a visiting Justice. We this day visited the Gaol in question. The prisoners were allowed to complain of being allowed only half a pound of bread for dinner with the exception of Tuesday's and Friday's. The only reply in our power to give them was that the dieting was under consideration, and that the result would be made known as soon as possible.

I. O. Travers
Visiting Justice.

A receipt for emptying the necessary at the Gaol - 1787 still exists today, and can be seen below. (The necessary being human waste.) Per 11th April 1787 of Mr. Richard White, Chamberman of the Borough of Portsmouth; Three Pounds Four Shillings, (£3-20P in today's money) for emptying the sewers of the Gaol. The receipt is Signed and marked with a cross by the Chamberman.

In 1877 a new prison, designed by G. Rake, architects, and built by H & W Evans of Portsmouth was opened, for the Borough Gaol had become outmoded and too small to keep up with the fast growing population. Due to this population increase the crime rate grew with it, and in turn, the Assize Court Judges dished out tough sentences. One other major factor concerning the rise in crime and the need for a new prison, was the ending of transportation to the Colonies in 1868.

The new prison was built at the junction between Milton

Road and St. Mary's Road in the Kingston district of Portsmouth. It is possible that a gallows was erected at the junction, for St Mary's Road was known as 'Dead Man's' Lane. This may have influenced the site of the prison.

The foundation stone was laid by the then Mayor, Alderman, G.E. Kent, (1874). He used a silver builder's trowel to ensure the stone was in the position it occupies today. On February 17th, 1999, the same trowel was auctioned by Sotheby's at Billinghurst, and bought by the City of Portsmouth to be added to the civic collection. The trowel has an unusual border of scrolling leaves around an inscription, which states. 'Used by the Mayor of Portsmouth on the occasion of laying the foundation stone of the New Gaol.'

The Governor of Kingston (1999) had hoped the Mayor of Portsmouth would repeat the same ceremony, using the same trowel used by Alderman G.E. Kent over 125 years ago, but this has not been ascertained. The intention was to dislodge the foundation stone, have it cleaned and the words and date re-carved before being replaced by the Mayor sometime during the millennium. It was also envisaged that a Time Capsule would be placed behind the foundation stone so that future historians will know more about Kingston's past.

The prison, when constructed, had approximately 32 cells for women and 139 cells for men. There was also a Governor's quarters, a workshop, eight punishment cells, a bakehouse, three reception cells and a chapel. (The chapel ceiling still retains its former glory, albeit hidden behind a modern false ceiling above where the new hospital was, (known as 'E' Wing.) The chapel was considered to be a fine place of worship and there a large gallery existed for female prisoners and a double entry at the sides for males. The back of the seats were slightly raised and must have been uncomfortable to sit on. The officers' didn't fare much better for their 'scats' were ugly and prominent.

In 1970 a new complex was constructed and a new chapel built on the second floor of this complex. However, after a severe arson attack by a disgruntled prisoner a major part of the complex was gutted by fire.

The dining hall and stage were the worst affected. The chapel on the floor above the dining hall was severely damaged by thick, black smoke, which could be seen for miles around. It was said that the fire began on the stage and quickly spread throughout the dining hall. The sheer skill and bravery of the City of Portsmouth's professional fire fighters thwarted the destruction of the kitchen.

The fire, it was alleged, was started by a prisoner named Hall who is reputed to have hated the prison to such an extent that he wanted out at any cost. Hall is still in prison after serving more than thirty years.

After this fire attack the chapel was moved into a partitioned area in the middle shop, now a storeroom for paper. Rumour had it that the chapel will once again be moved into one of the old television rooms off the centre, or even back into the middle shop, but this has not been decided yet. Moreover, the stage was rebuilt in another part of the dining hall; it once stood where the canteen was prior to closing.

'A' Wing's construction differed from 'C' and 'D' wings, for part of 'A' Wing was partitioned in 1885. Some of the windows in the cells on this wing were larger than the ones on other wings. These windows were specially incorporated for prisoners who suffered from TB, and for women who were pregnant.

Male prisoners occupied cells facing 'B' wing and had frosted glass panes so that the convicted men could not gaze on the women during their exercise period.

The other side of the partitioned off area was reserved for female prisoners. However, there were three small apartments here that accommodated female officers. Female prisoners used the recesses at the end of 'A' Wing which was later converted into an additional cell; (1999).

The left-hand side of the basement ('A' One, Annex) was for males. A stair led down here from the female officers' quarters to the laundry, which was situated in the basement on the right hand side and contained a copper boiler and nine washing tubs.

The kitchen occupied the north side between C and D wings and is roughly where it is today. A spiral staircase led downwards to the central hub basement from an adjoining gallery that encircled this central hub. A new floor was added here when the prison was refurbished prior to opening as a Borstal Recall Centre.

There was also a boiler house here and this was used to heat the entire building. One is still able to see where the spiral staircase wound its way up through the central hub and abutted on to the third floor landing.

A mortuary was built in 1907 behind the brickmaking workshop, which was on the right hand side after entering the prison yard from the Gatehouse. Any prisoner who died in the prison was taken to the local mortuary, and after an autopsy, the body was released to relatives.

Each Wing was, and still is 13 cells long. 'B' Wing was originally built as a one-story building. On one side was the prison hospital and the other side accommodated female prisoners. The education department (above), and the gymnasium (at the end of the wing), were later additions. Part of this wing now houses the prison's Security Department and probation offices. Rumour had it that these departments would be moved to the new complex, which was under refurbishment, (March 1999), and that the Security Department area would be turned into cell accommodation.

'C' Wing is the only wing that does not have a basement. This wing once accommodated male prisoners. Its level differs slightly, for there are a few steps, which lead down from the main central hub. At the end of this wing there is an entrance that goes into the present day workshops. Whereas before the same entrance led out to the dreaded treadwheel. (More on this later).

'D' Wing, the last of the wings had been home for some fifty lifers until the closure of the prison. This wing has not changed all that much since it was built. It is worth mentioning that none of the cell doors in Kingston had steel-backs when it was built. It is also interesting to know that an emergency telephone connected the prison with the town exchange; and it proved to be very effective in times of trouble.

Before 1909 digital cameras were not available to take the 'Mug Shots' of Debtors or Convicts. No studio where prisoners would be ordered to stare at a given point on a brick wall, no flash guns or identification cards. Therefore, convicts were taken outside into an open yard on the right hand side of the gatehouse, and there placed on a chair in front of a huge box-like camera that stood precariously on tripod legs. Then, amid a grey puff of smoke the prisoners' faces were frozen in a state of fear for posterity.

The prison changed considerably when it was taken over by the Government. Total cost of the construction of the prison came to £37,000. The Corporation was somewhat aggrieved over this, as they still had to bear the construction costs many years later.

A treadwheel was sited inside a red brick building in a corner of the main exercise area, (where the outside toilets are now and immediately on the other side of the wall which runs alongside the main London to Portsmouth railway line). And there, on a chocolate coloured door, the words, 'Wheel House' were painted in six-inch letters. On entering the 'Wheel House' one would have heard a dull grinding sound: for the wheel was geared on to millstones that ground corn into flour. The resulting product was supplied to other prisons in the County of Hampshire.

The building was approximately thirty feet long by fifteen feet wide. On the left hand side was where the Treadwheel was sited; not one, but four of them stood in two tiers divided by a gallery running the whole length of the building. The wheels were separated by a section of brick wall and divided into compartments, cutting each prisoner off from the other. The main object of this was to further implement the rule of silence.

At one end of the 'Wheel House' a gong was fixed to the wall and near it a brass disc swung like the pendulum of a clock. Every fifteen minutes the pendulum struck a bell and the officer in charge sung out something like; 'A1, B1, C1, D1.'

As each letter and number was called out, one of the prisoners stepped from the wheel on to stilt-like steps immediately behind his compartment and thankfully took his place on a seat, which was vacated by another prisoner.

The regulations at Kingston stated that each man had to spend fifteen minutes on the wheel and five minutes off it. The Treadwheel was in use at Kingston up until 1912. A model of a similar treadwheel is on display in the prison Boardroom and a photograph can be seen in the City Records Office and Museum at Portsmouth.

Other forms of punishments meted out at Kingston were tough and degrading; for prisoners had to complete stints on the Crank Wheel. The Crank Wheel was a box-like contraption perched on top of an iron pedestal. From this box jutted a handle and this handle had to be cranked until a given number of revolutions were attained.

When it became too easy to turn, the prisoner had to call out 'Screw'. This call alerted one of the patrolling officers to go and tighten a screw on the Crank, hence the sobriquet, 'Screw' for prison officers of today.

Picking Oakum was another degrading punishment detested by all prisoners. This entailed teasing out pre-weighed, short lengths of tarred hemp rope, which, when teased was used to line the timbers of ships' hulls. Many a fingernail was broken trying to accomplish this task.

A convicted prisoner, depending on what class he was, would be expected to complete one of the following three combined tasks. (This did not include the treadwheel).

A. Turn the crank 14,500 times and pick 110 pounds of oakum per day.

B. Turn the crank 12,500 times and pick 6 ounce of oakum per day.

C. Turn the crank 10,500 times per day.

These particular forms of mindless and degrading tasks were performed in the cells where the prisoners' had to eat and sleep. Eventually the above mentioned tasks were phased out, and other, more constructive work implemented.

The gatehouse was enlarged in 1902, by adding sleeping accommodation on the South inner side. In the past, HM Prison Kingston has served as a Royal Naval Detention Centre, a training school for the Portsmouth Constabulary, a storage area, and a Borstal recall centre. Finally, after extensive refurbishing in 1970 it opened as a prison for men convicted of domestic related murders.

Today, the prison accommodates lifers who have been convicted of various offences that carry a life sentence - and as far as is known, Kingston was the only prison in Europe, if not the world that accommodated men serving only life sentences. The first ten arrived at Kingston from Wormwood Scrubs on the 15th July 1970 - over the next twenty-eight years more than a thousand lifers have passed through Kingston's formidable gates.

Rules and Orders of Kingston Prison

Of the town of Portsmouth and County of Hampshire Established for the better Government. Pursuant to the STATUTE 32d GEO. 11d Chap. 28th.

Article 1

If the Gaoler, Turnkey or other officer or any prisoner, require or demand any money from a prisoner at his entrance, either for Garnish, Chamber Money, Cards, seeing Lucy Tower, or on any other pretence whatever, such persons, if a prisoner, shall have no share of the Corporation Box for one month; and if the Gaoler, Turnkey, or other officer, he shall forfeit to the Debtors fund, Five Shillings, and return the money so obtained from the prisoner.

II
Every Debtor shall retire quietly to his chamber between Lady Day and Michaelmas, at nine in the evening; between Michaelmas and Lady Day at eight; and it shall be optional for him to retire sooner; the out-doors shall be opened between Lady Day and Michaelmas at six in the morning, and between Michaelmas and Lady Day at seven.

III
For the better keeping of good order; no stranger shall be permitted to view the inside of the gaol without paying the officer attending, three pence; nor to play within the walls of the prison, unless in company with the debtors, or with their permission.

IV

The gaoler and his officers shall treat the several prisoners in his custody with tenderness and humanity; and the prisoners on their part, shall behave to them with decency and submission.

V

Any prisoner who shall abuse, insult, or ill treat the gaoler, turnkey, or any other person in the gaol, shall forfeit two shillings and sixpence, for every such offence; and if the gaoler or turnkey abuse, insult, or ill treat any prisoners, he shall forfeit the like sum for each offence.

Vl

If any prisoner shall have just cause of complaint against the gaoler, or any of his assistants, the same shall be made to the Inspector; and if the grievance be not redressed, to the next Quarter Sessions of the peace.

Vll

The gaoler, or turnkey, shall at all times within the stated hours attend at the door, and shall not unreasonably refuse the admission of persons enquiring for debtors.

VIII

Debtors may send for their necessaries, at all convenient times in the day, without hindrance or molestation. But the gaoler may restrain his prisoners from the use of ale, or strong beer for the purpose only of preventing drunkenness and disorder; but on no account shall exercise this authority unless occasioned by the improper conduct of the prisoners.

IX

If any charities be bestowed on the prisoners the gaoler shall carefully avoid partiality in the distribution of them, and divide them with much equality as possible.

X

Every prisoner who shall attempt, or assist in an escape, shall be committed to close confinement; but no debtor shall be confined in an unusual place or manner, except by the order of the Inspector, or of the Justices, or for a breach of those rules, as herein directed.

XI
If a clergyman attends the prison, due reverence and respect shall be paid to him; and every prisoner who is able, shall attend divine service; and any person who shall be guilty of indecent or improper behaviour during the service, shall, for the first offence, be confined, if a debtor, to his or her chamber for one week; and if a felon, to his cell; for the second offence a fortnight; and for the third offence, one calendar month.

XII
Care shall be taken at all convenient opportunities to open the windows of the gaol, particularly in the felons rooms, and all the passages, in order to admit fresh air, and preserve the health of the prisoners; and the felons shall be brought to the felons yard, and continue there at least three hours every day, when the weather will permit, and no candles, or other lights or fire, shall be admitted into any of the prisoners cells; none of the debtors or felons wives, children, or other of their families shall be permitted to live in the gaol.

XIV
If it be found necessary or requisite from the state or condition of any prisoner, such prisoner, shall as often as convenient, be bathed and cleansed in the bath belonging to the gaol, and the clothes of every prisoner shall be aired and cleansed in the hot oven, and particularly before they are brought to court.

XV
The debtor's common room passages and stairs shall be swept out daily by the debtor called the constable, or at her or his expense, the debtor who came in last to be the constable.

XVI

The felons tubs &c. shall be emptied and cleansed at eight o'clock in winter, and seven in summer, or sooner.

XVII

No prisoner, or other person, shall throw ashes, rubbish, or other dirt into any part of the yard, except in such places as shall be appointed by the Gaoler for that purpose; nor make water against any part of the building, under penalty of forfeiting for each offence; if a prisoner, four pence, if any other person, sixpence.

XVIII

No person shall play quoits, skittles, or other games that may injure the grass, or the garden on the front or west side of the building, but shall confine the amusements to the east side; and to avoid gaming. Any person playing for, or winning money at any game shall forfeit one shilling for every such offence.

XIX

Each convict shall be confined in a separate cell, and the several prisoners of different sexes shall, as much as possible, be kept apart from each other.

XX

No prisoner shall be obliged to sleep with one that is diseased.

XXI

No dog, or cat, or poultry shall be kept in the Gaol by any prisoner.

XXII

Whoever shall see or be informed of any of these rules being broken, or any other offence of any of the prisoners, shall give immediate notice of it to the Inspector, or in his absence, to the Gaoler.

XXIII

All fines and forfeitures imposed by these rules and orders on the debtors and others, except felons, shall be kept in a box secured with two locks and fixed in the debtor's day room for the sole purpose of purchasing such necessaries as may be agreed upon by a majority of the debtors, for use of their day room, and such instruments as they may think necessary for their reasonable amusement and exercise; the keys of the box to be kept by two persons to be appointed by such majority, and the forfeits of the felons to be laid out by the Gaoler, in butchers meat for their use.

XXIV

If any prisoner refuse or neglect for the space of one hour, to pay the penalty or forfeiture incurred as abovementioned every such prisoner shall immediately be committed to close confinement, and a diet of bread and water for forty eight hours.

These rules and orders to be hung up in the Gaoler's common kitchen and a copy in every common day room in the said Gaol. These rules applied to all prisons in Hampshire it is known they were in force at the old prion in Penny Street—then were probably the rules at Kingston, but it will give the reader an insight as to how tough prisons were in times gone by.

Table of Fees

For the lodging and board of each prisoner per week…£0 7s 0d
For each prisoner when he has a room and bed of the Gaoler and diets himself, per week £0 2s 0d For each prisoner when he finds own bed and diet, per week £0 0s 6d. To the Turnkey for the same £0 14s 0d. For the discharge of each prisoner. £0 13s
If two or more debtors lie in the same bed, to be paid amongst them weekly. £0 2s 6d

Every prisoner that will eat with the Gaoler to pay for his diet, three meals a day, per week. £0 4s 6d
For a copy of every commitment, if demanded. £0 1s 0d
For every certificate of order to a Habeas Corpus. £0 2s 6d
For the copy of every Sheriffs Warrant, if demanded. £0 1s 0d
For signing every certificate in order to obtain Superfedeas,
Or a rule or Order of the Court. £0 2s 6d

THE GAOLER is to take notice that by the 32d. GEO IIc 28s he shall not directly nor indirectly take of any prisoner for debt, damages, costs, or contempt any other fee for his commitment or coming to the Gaol, chamber rent there, release or discharge, than shall be allowed in the said Table of Fees, on pain to forfeit for every such offence (exclusive of the penalties inflicted by former laws, to the party grieved FIFTY POUNDS with treble costs.

We His Majesty's Justices of the Peace for the Town of Portsmouth and County of Hampshire assembled at the General Quarter Sessions of the Peace held in and for the said Town and County, have examined the above Rules and Orders, with the Table of Fees there underwritten, and to allow, and confirm the same.

What would prisoners of today think about paying for their bedding and meals. It certainly would not cost them a paltry few shillings, but several thousand pounds. Food for thought?

Diet for Prisoners Employed on the Treadmill.

The following diet tables are usual for prisoners in general and for those taking part in the treadmill; as one can see the diets are very different from what prisoners expect in this day and age. Nevertheless, all prisoners were fed according to a diet laid out by the prison doctor. There was no such diet as five pieces of fruit a day, or for that matter various choices of meals, including puddings. Men operating the treadmill were given extra rations, for they were doing physical work-related punishment.

Sunday; Breakfast; One quart oatmeal pottage half pound of bread. Dinner; One quart of stew of heads and bones etc. with half pound of bread. Supper; As breakfast.

Monday; Breakfast; As Sunday. Dinner; As Sunday. Supper; As breakfast.

Tuesday; Breakfast; As Sunday. Dinner; As Sunday. Supper; As breakfast.

Wednesday; Breakfast; As Sunday. Dinner; 5oz beef without bone after boiling 1lb potatoes and half pound of bread.

Thursday; Breakfast; As above Dinner; Three quart of broth of yesterday etc. Half pound bread with suitable vegetables and 6 oz flour made into a dumpling. Supper; As breakfast

Friday; Breakfast; As Sunday. Dinner; As Wednesday. Supper; As Breakfast.

Saturday; Breakfast, As above, Dinner As Monday, Supper, as above .

Diet Table 8th February 1837; For Prisoners in General.

Sunday; Breakfast; One quart of oatmeal pottage, half a pound of bread. Dinner; One quart of stew of heads and bones etc. with half pound of bread. Supper; As Breakfast

Monday; Breakfast; As above, Dinner; One quart oatmeal pottage, half pound of bread. Supper; As Breakfast.

Tuesday; Breakfast; As above, Dinner; As Monday. Supper; As Breakfast

Wednesday; Breakfast; As above, Dinner; 5oz beef without bone after boiling 1lb potatoes and half pound of bread Supper; As breakfast

Thursday; Breakfast; As above Dinner; 5oz. Beef without bone after boiling 1lb potatoes. Supper; As breakfast.

Friday; Breakfast; As above Dinner; Quart of broth from beef of yesterday etc. half pound of bread with leeks or onions and a quarter oz of oatmeal or each prisoner. Supper; As breakfast

Saturday; Breakfast; As above, Dinner; As Monday. Supper; As above.

8th February 1837
By The Clerk of the peace.

The Changing Face Of Kingston Prison

In 1983 there was a growing number of exceptionally violent prisoners being held in various segregation units in the Southeast area. Consequently, Kingston Prison's punishment block was converted into a top security special unit for selected troublemakers. These tough prisoners came to Kingston for a twenty-eight-day lie-down.

The first batch arrived from Albany on the Isle of Wight on 22nd June 1983, the last one on the 25th September 1986. Over three years Kingston accommodated forty-one special prisoners. It is fair to state that not one officer in the prison received any injuries during this time.

The unit closed on the 8th October 1986. The cell accommodation at Kingston today consists of three adjoining wings, marked A, C, and D. The hospital wing ('E' wing) accommodated lifers over the age of 55, but the majority were over 60 years old. Each wing had two landings and there was a small annex, which held 14 prisoners. The annex, which was enlarged in 1996 and situated in the basement of 'A' wing.

The whole prison accommodated up to 196 prisoners and every cell had its own sanitation, including hot and cold running water and in-cell electrical points.

There is also a six-cell segregation unit in 'A' wing basement, which is rumoured to have had so many cobwebs that a film company offered to buy them for a horror production. It is here that mandatory drug tests were carried out on a random basis.

The daily regime routine was as such the prisoners were unlocked at 0750, and locked up at 2100. The prison had 4 television rooms, one of which was used for the showing of videos. This has since changed, for prisoners' on the enhanced regime were able to rent a colour television set for as little as £1 per week from the prison authorities.

Association was mainly in the form of playing pool or snooker and there was one pool table on each wing and a snooker table sat astride the central hub, known as the centre.

Facilities existed for outside recreation, and on Saturdays and Sundays. Visiting football teams were allowed inside the prison to participate in competitive sport. The prison football team, (Kingston Arrows), were always in a good position in the league table and won awards and cups in the past. There is a book 'Manslaughter United' which concerns the team.

The visiting room, which was built on the site of an old brickmaking shop, has since been demolished and in its place an administrative block erected. On the ground floor of this building a new visiting room was constructed. Rules, however, were relaxed somewhat and inmates no longer had to wear prison clothing when going on a visit.

However, other major changes were implemented in the visiting room. New chairs and low coffee tables were introduced, and in due course they were bolted to the floor. Two raised platforms became a new feature so that staff could see everything that went on, especially drug smuggling. It seemed that the CCTV camera was not adequate enough to counter drug smuggling into Kingston.

Eventually the visit's canteen was transformed into a closed visiting area and drinks and cake could only be purchased from a vending machine fixed permanently to a wall. Whereas before visitors purchased tea and cakes and carried them over to the prisoner at the table. Even prisoners themselves could go to the canteen and purchase whatever they wanted and pay for the goods by signing a book and that cost was deducted from the prisoner's wages the following week.

Kingston Physical Recreation Department was probably one of the best in the prison system. Three instructors were available and any inmate could join in the programme, which consisted of Badminton, Volleyball, a weight room, and several outside interests, including; Football, Hockey, Bowls and running.

The prison library, although small, was well stocked with

over 6,000 books and talking tapes. A librarian from Portsmouth library visited on a weekly basis.

Plans to build a geriatric ward (E Wing), in the old administrative area was implemented in 1995 and completed in 1997. This part of the prison was run on the lines of an old people's home - a place to care for lifers who may never be released back into society and known internally as 'Death Row'. This wing also housed the prison Health Care Centre.

The Education Department was superb and geared up to the changing needs and interests of the prison population. 'O' and 'A' level standards were available in all subjects, including Maths and English. There were several places on Information Technology, Psychology, Music, Upholstery, Yoga, General Studies, Creative Writing classes and Assertiveness and Decision Making Skills. However, due to Government cutbacks in the 1990's, Kingston Prison's educational needs were severely curtailed for a short time. Up until the prison closed the department was running as smooth as ever, owing to the perseverance and deliberation of Trevor Payne, head of education. (1985-1999). (More on Trevor Payne later).

There were three full-time probation officers who dealt with inmates and their various problems. Each officer was responsible for lifer reports, which were made out in time for F75 boards and Local Reviews. These F75 Boards and Local Reviews are still part of the on-going process of a lifer's Career Plan. This helped the authorities and the Parole Board to make recommendations for less secure conditions - or parole.

The Kingston Probation Department also liaised closely with the inmate's outside probation officer. This service included Alcohol and Drug awareness, education, Anger/Stress Management, and Relationship Skills Courses. Some new courses came on stream and were; Lifers Course For Lifers and (R&R), Reasoning and Rehabilitation. There was a small laundry within the prison, which dealt mainly with prisoners' private clothing - but any larger articles, sheets etc. were sent to HM Prison Ford. Soap powder was purchased from the prison's shop, along with many other requisites, and all from an average wage of £9 per week. Wages, like any other commodity, tend to fluctuate and some prisoners earned as much as £20 per week.

Prison related work.

There were three thriving workshops in the prison; Number 1 shop contained the computerised section of the prison's printing industry, where typesetting, plate-making and lithographic printing was the order of the day.

Number 2 shop catered for print finishers, and had a small, but unique bookbinding section where many a rare book has been bound with loving care. After the riots at Manchester Prison several historical books and document were charred, but these books and documents were sent to Kingston Prison and restored to their original condition by Kingston inmates.

Number 3 shop was where inmates learned the art of working in a drafting office, and skill courses in VTC training for Computer aided designs were taught. A City and Guilds Certificate was presented to all inmates who passed the required examinations.

Other jobs include domestic cleaners and kitchen orderlies, where around 20 inmates were employed. Ten inmates worked with the works maintenance team, especially tradesmen. The kitchen employed 8 men and the garden party 10.

All lifers who passed through Kingston were subject to a short internal induction period of around three days, during which the wing principle officer, education facilitator and probation officer interviewed them. After the prisoner has been in the prison for approximately three months he was released on a full-scale induction board. Each man was allocated a case officer who took special interest in the inmates under his care, advising and helping them in any way he could.

Frequent Lifer Review Boards were held in the prison, chaired by the Lifer Governor and attended by any staff concerned in the writing up of reports on the prisoner, who was present? These boards were generally held three months prior to an F75 report or L.R.C. report. They also offered help, and gave advice in which to address any problematical areas of concern. (Risk Factors).

Death of the Peacocks and attempted murder.

Incidentally, in the grounds of Kingston prison, three Peacocks once strutted around in defiance of all and sundry. Then suddenly on or about the 9th of July 1995 they were all found dead. It was recorded at the time that the birds woke inmates up early in the morning; and it was then easily deduced that a trusted inmate caught them and broke their necks - the birds were the Governors sole pride and joy.

Killing Peacocks wasn't the only crime committed behind the stout walls of Kingston Prison, and Governor's adjudication reports lay testimony to this. Several prisoners were charged with assault, attempted murder, arson, drug smuggling, making illicit alcohol, (hooch), and theft.

One prisoner, who shall remain nameless, tried to kill another prisoner by rigging up the bath with electric wire, which was jammed into an electrical socket. When the inmate stepped into the bath he received severe burns to his body. The nameless prisoner was taken to court, found guilty and sentenced to a further ten years imprisonment.

For several months inmates barracked the Governor to purchase shoe-racks for each wing. Resident Principle officer, (PO Le Conte) eventually managed to buy one for a testing period. The shoe-rack was placed on 'D' wing. No sooner had it been put there than it was immediately whisked away. After a couple of cell searches, the shoe-rack was found and returned to its proper station.

The 'nicked' inmate pleaded his case with the Governor; stating that he found it in a dustbin smashed in little pieces.

'I mended it and kept it for my own use,' he said. 'After all, possession is nine tenths of the law.'

The Governor made short shrift of this lame excuse, slapped the culprit's wrist and fined him £5; a usual form of punishment dished out at Kingston.

To continue with this Souvenir History of Kingston Prison I'd like to add some of the sentences handed down by Judges on those who committed some of the most atrocious offences against their fellow human beings; and cover some of the most daring escapes from the prison.

Crimes, Sentences and Escapes

Through the ages the prison has been used for men and women serving sentences for debt, and anything from a few days up to life imprisonment. There have been no executions in Kingston; all executions took place at Winchester. Here follows a list of offences committed and sentences handed down by the Judiciary of the day.

Gaming (pitch and toss). 1 month, or 27/-(£1.35p) fine.
Fortune telling. 7 days hard labour.
Desertion of wife. 1-3 months hard labour,
Desertion of wife and family. 3 months hard labour.
Neglect of children. 1 month hard labour.

Neglecting to send child to school. 7 days or 8/- fine (40p)
Sleeping out. 7 days to 1 month hard labour.
Begging. 14 days to 1 month hard labour.
Obscene language. 1 month hard or 44/6 (£2-23p) fine.
Assault on male (given to female). 2 month hard labour.
Stealing rabbit skin, and bone. 1 month hard labour.
Attempting to steal one penny. 14 days hard labour.
Possession of 'unreasonable' salmon. 1 month or
£5/10/6 fine, (£5.53).
Refusing workhouse task. 21 days hard labour.
Deserting workhouse with clothes. 1 month or 41/- (£2.0.5.) fine.

Of course the more serious offenders were either executed or transported to the colonies for long periods, and that included life.

It is impossible to say how many convicts escaped from Kingston; for no true figure exists anymore. Below however, are some unusual tales of those who did escaped, and of their daring exploits. One prisoner, according to Warder W Jacobs, escaped from custody before arriving at Kingston and was on the run for four days, only to be caught and returned to serve his time at the prison.

Warder Jacobs also describes an exciting escape when a postman was arrested for stealing letters. He was sentenced at Lewes Assizes and transported from there to Portsmouth by train. When his guard looked out of the train window, the prisoner slipped his handcuffs, jumped from the train and vanished across the fields.

One other escape concerning Kingston prison was when a prisoner made good his escape from the horse-drawn Black Maria that brought him to the prison gates. He ran across the fields, (Kingston Prison area was still countryside at the time), and if it were not for the quick action of a prison guard the man would have made good his escape.

The guard unhitched one of the horses that drew the Black Maria, and after a splendid display of bareback riding the prisoner was re-captured.

One man cheekily sawed through the hinges of his cell door, and when the guard slid back the bolt in the morning the door fell from its hinges with a resounding crash. The guard couldn't believe his eyes, especially when he was confronted with an empty cell for the prisoner had done a runner and vanished into thin air.

When the prisoner was eventually captured, he was asked how he managed to saw off the hinges. The man smiled contemptuously when he produced a new white-handled table knife. Now the guards wondered where he got the knife. He explained that it was brought into the prison inside a cake, (so all those jokes concerning knives and files hidden in cakes really are true).

In the modern age, not many men have made good their escape, most being caught before they have sawed partway through the cell bars.

One man did manage to get over the wall; John Hilton, a lifer, escaped from custody in 1992. He was sentenced to life imprisonment for the Mitcham Dairy murder. He served 11 years and was released on licence. He committed further offences and was given a further 18 years in prison, therefore re-activating his life sentence. Kingston was deemed a fairly secure place to send him; (he was sixty years old by this time, but Hilton thought of nothing else but that of escaping).

Within a couple of years he made his getaway with outside help. Hilton managed to wangle his way into obtaining a job in the prison kitchen. Part of this job was to empty the kitchen offal into a container provided by the local council. Hilton noticed that he was allowed into the prison yard for as long as it took him to complete the job. He immediately cottoned-on that the head chef and the patrolling officer gave him lots of leeway.

In due course Hilton planned his escape during domestic visits. That plan was to have an accomplice throw a rope over the prison wall on the same side where the railway line runs along the length of wall, a short distance from the kitchen. This was done and Hilton sprinted across to the foot of the wall and made good his escape.

It was an unusual escape, unusual because John Hilton had some fingers missing on one of his hands. So climbing the rope must have been very difficult for him. That though was not the end of the story; for when Hilton was at large he committed another armed robbery in London's Bond Street.

John Hilton is still in prison and was a category 'A' man for many years. He is now in a category 'C' establishment and it is doubtful if he will be released unless a new law is evoked.

During the middle of year 2000 Mick Bailey, a double murderer of two teenage girls was charged with smuggling £1,500 into the prison to purchase drugs. The Rev George Sands, retired, was also charged. Sands, of Portsmouth Elm church was bailed pending further enquiries into the illicit trade of drugs into the prison.

This is similar to the illicit trade of whisky and tobacco smuggling into the prison by Nuns. One of the sisters, who had been visiting prisoners for over thirty years was banned from visiting the prison and other nuns have to see prisoners in the company of a prison officer.

Formal Caution; 1837

**When a prisoner was discharged from prison he was given
a caution as below;
7th & 8th Geo IV c 28 Sec 11.**

Whereas it is expedient to provide for more exemplary punishment of offenders who commit felony, after a previous conviction for felony, whether such conviction shall have taken place before or after the commencement of this Act; Be it therefore enacted, that if any person shall commit any felony not punishable with death, committed after a previous conviction for felony such person shall on subsequent conviction, be liable (at the discretion of the court) to be transported beyond the seas for life or any term not less than seven years, or to be imprisoned for any term not exceeding four years; and if male, to be once, twice or thrice publicly or privately whipped (if the court shall so think fit) in addition to such imprisonment.

Modern Day Caution 2013

Establishment..

Prison No...

Surname...
Forenames...

Sentence...
Section 21 Firearms Act 1968; Certificate (As amended By S29 C.J.A. 1972)

I understand that I am not allowed to possess, or have anything to do with firearms or ammunition of any description, ***for the rest of my life/for a period of five years from discharge/for the duration of my licence**.

*(Cross out inapplicable)

I understand my rights of appeal to the **Crown court (Scotland, Sheriff)** in the area of my abode.

Punishments for contravention are;

> (a) Summary Conviction, 6 months imprisonment, a fine, **OR BOTH.**
> (b) On Indictment, 3 years imprisonment, a fine, **OR BOTH.**

Prisoner (Signature)..

Date..

Officer (Signature)..

Officer Name..

(Block Capitals).

Location and date lower portion sent.

F2050 F This portion to be retained by the establishment.

Above; Kingston Prison Clock tower.

Below; Prisoner being restrained prior to being flogged.

Above; The segregation cell at Kingston, which was hardly used.

Below; a typical cell in the early 1960's.

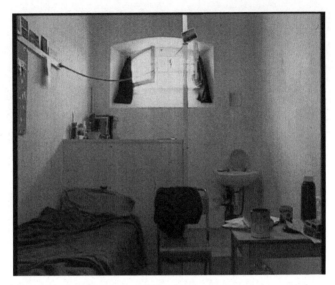

Above; Typical cell up to 2013.

Below; Prisoners on the tread wheel.

Above; A prisoner on the Crank.

Below; A view of the Gatehouse from the outside.

Above; boys as young as twelve were imprisoned.

Below; Prisoner prepared for birching.

F1145 – Explanation of Procedure at Disciplinary Charge Hearings.

1   This note tells you what happens when you appear before the governor at a disciplinary charge hearing. The prisoners' Information Pack sets out the legal rules about discipline. The Manuel on the Conduct of Adjudications also gives guidance on procedure, and you can ask to see a copy. Ask an officer if you want more advice in advance.

2   The governor will ask you;

(a)   If you have received the notice of report (F1127) showing the charge (s against you.

(b)   If you have received this card and you understand how the hearing will proceed. Say if you do not understand anything.

3 The Charge (s will be read out and the governor will ask if you understand them. Say if you do not, or if they are different from those on the notice of report.

4 The governor will ask you;

If you have written a reply to the charge (s

If you have had enough time to prepare your answer or defence. If you feel you have not, say why. The governor can then decide whether to adjourn the hearing.

If you want any additional help at the hearing and if you do, you should say whether you should like to have legal assistance by a friend or adviser or legal representation. It is for the governor to decide whether or not legal representation can be agreed in your case. If refused, the hearing will continue and you should be ready for this. However, if agreed, the hearing may be adjourned so that you can contact a solicitor. The legal aid officer can help you.

If you want to call any witnesses, and if so whom. You can also ask for witnesses later, when the time comes to give your defence or explanation (see 10-11 below). But if you give the names now, the governor will have more time to find them and call them to give evidence.

Whether you plead guilty or not guilty to each separate charge. If you are still unsure why you have been charged you should plead not guilty. You will be treated as pleading not guilty unless you plead guilty.

5 The officer who reported you will give evidence. You can then question the officer on the evidence or any relevant matter.

6 Any witnesses in support of the Charge (s against you will then give evidence, and you can question them. Do not argue with witnesses. If you cannot put the right questions to bring out your point, ask the governor to help you.

7 If you have pleaded not guilty the governor will then ask you to make your defence to the charges.

8 If you have pleaded guilty, the governor will invite you to explain your conduct.

9 You can now read out any written statement you have made in your defence or explanation. If you prefer, the governor will read it out for you.

10 If you want to call witnesses, ask if you can do so and say who they are, even if you have already named them. If they are in your defence, say what you believe their evidence will prove. If the governor is satisfied that they may help establish what happened, they will be called. Remember that other prisoners cannot be forced to give evidence.

11 You, and others present, can question the witnesses on their evidence or any relevant matter.

12 Whether or not you have called witnesses, you can now say anything further about your case, comment on the evidence and point out anything you think is in your favour.

13 The governor will announce a finding of guilty or not guilty for each charge.

14 If you are found guilty, the governor, before awarding any punishment, will invite you to say why you think you should be treated leniently. You can ask to call someone to support a plea for leniency.

15 A report will be read out on your conduct and your record since you last came into custody. The governor will ask whether you want to add anything or ask any questions about the report.

16 The governor will announce the punishment s) for each offence proved. If you do not understand how the punishment will affect you, ask the governor to explain.

17 The governor may adjourn the hearing or bring it to an end at an early stage. This could be, for example, to await the result of police investigations, or so that a key witness can be present. You will be told the reason. You will be returned to your normal location unless you are being segregated under prison Rule 43 or Young Offender Institution Rule 46.

F1145 (revised 4/92)

Adjudication Information for the Governor.

No. 00001
Bw1910

Name Blank
Name deleted
Length of sentence
Life
Date of sentence
08 04 93
Date of arrival at Maidstone
03 02 97
Wing located in
A Wing
Total number of offences against discipline
21
Total number at Kingston
7
Date of last report
01 06 98
Any of a similar type
7
Any suspended sentence
nil
NPD
n/a
Work area
Print Shop
Average wage
£9.00
Incentive level
Standard

Record of Hearing and Adjudication; F256

Part I to be completed in block capitals before hearing.
The Establishment's name is given;
The date of adjudication;
Prisoner's name and number and what sentence he is serving, in
this case the prisoner is serving a life sentence.
Details of the charge follows as recorded on F1127.

The prisoner was charged under Rule 47 paragraph 17, uses threatening, abusive, or insulting words or behaviour.

At approximately 13 04 hours, 30th July 1998, Weald wing cell 2/23 you threatened officer Blank by saying; 'If you want it – I'll fracking give it to you now.'

The F1127 was issued by officer Blank and the time and date was; 200. 00 hrs. 30/7/98. The reporting officer was officer Blank and his rank of officer.

The medical officer then ticks of the fit for adjudication and Fit for cellular confinement boxes. The medical officer then signs it and adds the date; 31/7/98.

The governor adjudicating then ticks off his box; in this case it was governor Hales. He then gives a reason why he is adjudicating and not the governing governor. Governor Blank said that the governor and Head of Custody were on annual leave.

The F254 Report is read out to the governor, which includes the prisoner's name, number, wing allocation and cell number. It is also dated. The offence committed is read out contrary to Rule 47 Para 17 Prison rules.

Officer's Report follows;
Sir,

At approximately 13 40 hours on the 30th of July 1998, I went to cell 2;23 on Weald wing to ascertain the nature of the noise and the call bell being pressed.

Inmate Blank (BW1910) confronted me about being banged up that afternoon and I told him that my orders from the wing PO were that he remained behind his door because he was not required for work.

He became threatening and abusive saying that he was going to 'Kick off' and said to me. 'If you want it – I'll fracking give it to you.' He said this in an in an extremely aggressive manner. Officer Blank was with me at the time and witnessed the whole incident. This, Sir, concludes my evidence.

The officer signed the report, dated it and added his rank.
Part 2 Preliminaries follows;

The time adjudication commenced is recorded; 09 40 hours.
The prisoner is identified and the following questions are asked.

Have you received the notice of report F1127?
Yes
Have you received F1145 explaining how this hearing will proceed?
Yes
Do you understand the procedure?
Yes
Charge is read out at this stage;
Do you understand the charge?
Yes
Have you made a written reply to the charge?
No
Have you had sufficient time to prepare your answer?
Yes
Do you want any additional help at this hearing?
No
Will you be calling any witnesses – Yes and No box was left blank.
How do you plead Guilty or Not Guilty, the Not Guilty box was ticked.

Part 3 Record of hearing;

Record of all salient points;

Officer's evidence read out.

Gov; 'Do you wish to question the evidence?

Inmate; 'I did kick the door and did ring the bell and I told him that I had been on bang up for about 9 weeks. I might as well be on basic.

Gov; Are you aware of the routine that if you are not working you remain in your cell.

Inmate; Yes. Some were watching TV, I'm depressed at the moment.

Part 4 Referral to Police;

The police were not involved in this case, so no boxes were ticked off.

If finding was one of guilt, prisoner's plea of mitigation; If none, state none.

I'm depressed and my mother is ill and my Auntie has only 2 years to live. I am waiting to attend the aggression control course.

A report on previous conduct during sentence is read out at this stage, which includes the number of previous findings of guilt; which was 21 in this case.

Does the prisoner wish to add anything more or ask any questions in connection with report?
The prisoner said no.

Part 6 Punishment;
Various punishments are rewarded; EG;

Caution; Forfeiture of remission / Award of added days; Prospective forfeiture
of remission/added days; confinement to room; Exclusion from

associated work; Stoppage of earnings; In this case the prisoner was fined £10 over a period of 1 month.

The remaining forfeiture of privileges is; no canteen, no association, no tobacco, no publications, no radio, in this case the prisoner was fined.

Are there any existing suspended punishments; In this case None.

Prisoner was informed of punishment and activation; yes.

The Governor then signed the Part 6 Punishment and dated it.

The officer presiding then added his signature; (A C Blank).

Sixty Days' Experience;
A Pathetic Story

It felt like only yesterday when I first met John Smith. He had just undergone two months imprisonment in Kingston Prison. He was of quiet demeanour and respectable in appearance; his face was a mite anxious and careworn, and looked about thirty five years old. I was attracted to him, and became interested in this man.

Clearly he had seen better days and I am sure he noticed my frequent glances to wards him. He made a sudden movement, which I took as a sign of resentment at my curiosity, and yet, while I turned my eyes away, and gazed into space, I was hoping he thought me as being a sympathetic person... for somehow I was convinced he had a story to tell.... A story that would interest me, and indeed those who would read it in the years to come.

A gentleman sitting nearby, who was known to me, had heard this story, or at least some of it, and I wanted the rest for my 'Brief History of Kingston Prison.' He nodded over in my direction and winked; I knew I was in and walked across the room towards John Smith, who would relate his experiences in Kingston Prison, and I set his words out below.

John Smith.... That is not his real name, but one I have given him to hide his true identity. John held a very responsible position in a Hampshire engineering company, which was taken over by another, much larger company. Because of this takeover, manpower cuts were inevitable and so it was that John Smith was made redundant. In the ensuing months he tried to find other work, therefore he had to earn his living by canvassing and peddling various goods up and down the country. He was not at all successful at this type of work and one miserable Monday morning he stole the cash he had earned for his firm, and was caught, convicted and sentenced by Portsmouth magistrates to undergo hard labour in Kingston Prison for sixty days.

First impressions of prison.

'While my memory is still fresh I shall never forget those sixty days, with humiliation and remorse, leavened with apprehensions as to the welfare of my wife and young children, and how I was to face the future. I could not restrain at any time during my imprisonment a passionate, almost frenzied grief, for my misdoings, which had brought penance and disgrace. After being sentence I was removed to the cells below, overcome and dazed with distress.

With five others I was taken in a van to the prison, and on the way they enquired of each other their sentences, their offences, and offered consolations, mingling with the latter with observations on their trials. We were taken into the receiving department, where the chief warder checked the entry book for our ages, religion, and sentences. Our clothes and property were taken from us, then we had a bath and then medically examined.'

'After this we had to change into prison garb, then placed in temporary cells and awarded a pint of thin gruel and a piece of wholemeal bread, called a loaf, but weighing only six ounces. This was my very first meal in prison. About an hour had passed and we were then marched, single file, into the prison proper. It was then that a warder read out the rules we had to observe. They were many and most bewildering. Afterwards we were given our numbers, and told to go to our cells. I walked on, not noticing the numbers, but a gruff voice yelled.' 'Now then, you. You didn't know... not bin in 'ere before? Well, now you turn round and look at that, and don't forget it!'

'A minute more and the iron doors slammed shut on me, and I saw the inside of a prison cell for the first time. It was about twelve feet long by seven feet wide, and thirty six whitewashed bricks high. The furniture was a stool, a plank in the corner, a tin dust pan, and a washing bowl, a pannakin (jug) for water, and a small table.' Some prisoners even wore masks lest they should contaminate warders and visitors with the evil eye.

Plank Bed Miseries.

'When in the solitude of my cell I was determined to do my best to satisfy prison requirements. Presently a warder came along and said; 'Now then, don't you know it's bed time?'

'Where's the bed'? I asked.

'There, up in the corner, don't you see? You're trying it on!'

I looked up in the corner at the plank, and I will now tell you what the bed is like. 'There were three pieces of board about a quarter of an inch apart, and three together about twenty inches wide by six feet. It might have been a good plank when it was new, but the two outside ones were higher than the ones in the middle, so that it just caught one in the small of the back. For a pillow, another piece of wood was nailed on at the head. However, I took the bed down and stripped off my clothes, laid a sheet on the plank and then rolled myself up in a blanket and quilt. It was bitter cold and I got no sleep. When the first bell rang in the morning I was right joyful, though my bones were so sore I could scarcely walk. Believe me when I say that, I never got more that two hours sleep in all the time I spent in prison, except for once, but I often got up in the middle of the night to walk about and stamp my feet and shake myself, lest I froze to death.'

Prison Work Routine.

'By six o'clock my cell had to be swept and tidied, bed clothes neatly folded and arranged on the plank, and my hands and face washed. Then came an old hand to instruct me how to pick oakum. I did my best to learn, but I'm afraid I was a bad scholar. Oakum consists of old tarred ropes, and to pick it, 'As fine as your hair.' as the warder says, is a difficult task, a heart breaking job. Just before eight o'clock you get your breakfast, half a pint of gruel and six ounces of bread.'

'After the meal, all bed clothes have to be neatly rolled together, roly-poly fashion and then there is a service in the chapel for half an hour. Next to your cell, clean tins with brick and rags, and pick oakum. About ten o'clock you are ordered to exercise on fine days. The exercise consists in walking round rings in the yard for an hour at a distance of three or four feet from each other, for I needn't tell you, this is the silent system. But the silence is broken. A regular gaolbird put his hand to his mouth as if to pull his beard, and in something between a whisper and a mutter said; 'You're a green 'un, I can see that. How long have you got, matey? Two months? Why didn't you get six months, you fool! They'll starve you!'

'Back to your cell, after exercise, and more oakum picking. At twelve, dinner—four ounces of bread and six ounces of potatoes steamed in their skins. You are kept oakum picking for the rest of the day, with an interval for supper, which consists of six ounces of bread and a pint of gruel. At eight o'clock the bell rings for bed. That was the weary monotony of my prison life, with its half starving fare. Of course some prisoners have to break stones or make mats. These are preferable to oakum picking, which brings sleepless nights and long vigils with brain racking unspeakable memories.'

If John Smith was imprisoned in Kingston Prison in 1970 he would have had to have been sentenced to life imprisonment. He certainly would have seen the differences in the prison routine. He would also have been able to sleep in a proper bed with sheets and quilt. Yet he still would have moaned and whinged his way through his sentence.....

An Old Lag's Tale

Following on from John Smith's; 'Sixty Day's Experience,' I decided to venture into Kingston prison with the intention of living and updating his experiences, but it cost me 28 days of my own freedom. I did not have to get myself nicked, but all freelance reporters will go to any lengths to write his story; so I went in undercover, so to speak and with the Governor's blessing.

Within a couple of days I met Albert Cartwright (that's not his real name), when I was walking around the circles in the exercise yard. The same yard that was probably used by John Smith when he was imprisoned in Kingston.

Albert had so many alias's that he couldn't remember his real name. He was two years into an IPP life sentence for robbing a building society in Guildford, brandishing a loaded sawn-off shotgun and was sentenced at Winchester Assizes.

When I first clapped eyes on Albert he tended to put his hand across his lips as he spoke in low whispers out of one corner of his toothless mouth. A trick that was probably familiar to John Smith when prisoners spoke like this because the silent system denied prisoners the right to communicate with one another.

Lucky to get a short Tariff.

There was still a twinkle in Albert's piercing blue eyes. He told me that he once worked as a bank teller, but temptation got the better of him, and he robbed the building society where he worked. For the next twenty years or so he was in and out of various prisons for robbery. This time he was sentenced to an IPP in Kingston prison. Albert told me he was lucky for he could have been given a full life sentence, but the judge gave him an IPP with a 4 year tariff because of his age; Albert was in his 69th year.

He told me that he had a couple of good touches over the years, got married, then divorced, then managed to get back with his ex-wife.

'My wife cleared out and spent all the money I robbed from building societies' all over Hampshire. This was to be my last job, for my retirement, so to speak. But I was lucky to get such a short tariff. I'll do four years, maybe five, but look where I am now, banged up tight in this absolute hell hole. So you take my advice young 'un, don't ever come back. Do your time, reflect on the experience and listen to what I'm about to tell you....'

Heating in Kingston Prison.

'Many elderly prisoners complained about the heating in Kingston. Us older prisoners have to endure freezing conditions when the heating is switched off in April, and is not turned on again until October.'

Albert tells me that prisoners of his age group have a tendency to feel the cold more than the younger generation, and Kingston prison tends to be blasted by the icy winds coming in from the sea and howls up the railway line.

He also said that most of the time he spends his days in bed under the blankets. Every day is the same, regardless of the weather outside the wings; for the cells are freezing 24 hours a day. Therefore he is inclined to stay in bed more often than he does out of it; and he still has another 18 months left to finish off his sentence.

Albert told me that in March 2012 the prison was inspected by the Chief Inspector of Prisons—and lo and behold the heating was switched on for two whole days, then it was turned off when the inspection was over.

'Sometimes,' he says; 'The weather can bite straight through your very clothes and right into your skin.'

Yet Albert continues to battle with the elements. The only

time he can enjoy sitting in his cell is when the heating is turned on in October. He only leaves his cell for meals, exercise and a couple of hours on association in the evening.

The Future

It is known that rumours abound in penal establishments and that these rumours travel speedily down the prison grapevine. Some of these stories are true others completely false. Most should be taken with a pinch of salt for there is no truth in the rumour that Kingston prison is about to be turned into a female prison, or indeed into a Youth Custody Centre. However, it is possible that Kingston will revert to its original status as a local prison serving the Portsmouth district.

However, it is also conceivable that the prison might be used to accommodate foreign nationals who have found their way into Britain illegally.

Perhaps Haslar over at Gosport is earmarked to be turned into a huge housing and shopping complex as a portion of a re-generation plan. Part of that regeneration scheme may incorporate Haslar prison?

Adjudications of a Violent Prisoner.

Here follows a list of a prisoner's prison record from 1990 to 2006.

1990; Threats to other prisoners (it is documented that Mr.......
threatened to stab another prisoner with a pair of scissors).
1991; Assault on another prisoner which resulted in segregation.
1992; Assault on a prison officer.
1993; Smashed up his prison cell.
1993; Threats to kill staff and prisoners which resulted in a dirty protest.
1994; Assault on another prisoner which resulted in him being removed from HMP Grendon.
1995; Threats of violence.
1996; Whilst at HMP Albany he caused £250 damage and threatened an officers life.
1999; Assaulted another prisoner whose injuries included a fractured jaw and other facial injuries.

2.7 I note that he also has the following adjudications that are an indication of poor behavioural control.;

08 05 00; Fighting.
26 11 03; Fighting.
13 10 03; Assaulting another prisoner.
02 08 04; Assaulting another prisoner.

His last adjudication was on 02 08 06 for disobeying a lawful order. The above record was put in front of a parole board hearing in October 2011 and guess what? The prisoner was granted parole, perhaps the Parole Board came to the conclusion that this particular prisoner would not be as violent in the community and granted him parole.

Zimmer Frame Society

The prison population in England continues to surpass all previous records on a daily basis. As this population hovers around the 90,000 mark and the learned judges continue to incarcerate and sentence people to unduly lengthy prison terms, can only add up to one thing; thousands of prison places will have to be found for a growing number of old and disabled prisoners.

These aged and infirm men and women, including many hundreds sentenced to life, will through time, suffer from various forms of disabilities. However, as this Zimmer frame society transgresses from the infirm to the completely disabled – then something will have to be done before it's too late.

So what is being done?

Why is the Prison Service preparing the old and disabled for the scrap heap? Is there another, better option in which to treat this forgotten society.

The Prison Service acknowledges that elderly and infirm prisoners are, and will be, a huge problem in the years to come. But, as is almost always the case, and the Prison Service will argue that there is not enough funding to pay for specialist equipment for those that have severe disabilities, other than what is required by law.

Sometimes though, cash can be found to convert existing buildings and transform them into accommodation for the disabled. This is what happened at H. M. Prison, Leyhill in Gloucestershire, which is a low security category 'D' establishment. For example, a ground floor spur on one of the wings was converted to house prisoners with disabilities.

Cell doors were enlarged for wheel chair users, shelves that held televisions were lowered and prisoners supplied with remote controls; in-cell lighting was adapted for those who have epilepsy and portable loop systems are available for those with impaired hearing.

There is also a new wing being constructed to accommodate elderly prisoners that will never be released into society and many of those prisoners have already been moved from Kingston prison awaiting a place at Leyhill.

The toilets, shower rooms and the general ablution areas were specially adapted. Emergency warning notices have been displayed on each cell door and a chair ramp constructed where once there was stairs.

However, it had taken four long years to raise the level of awareness of the disabled within the prison. It was as far back as 2003/2004 that the seeds were sown before the project was finally completed. As these seeds germinated into fruition another campaign was launched by Prison Officer Sue Sharples, who is the prison liaison officer for aged and disabled prisoners.

This new operation concerned the building of a conservatory, which would be attached to the newly converted wing and used as a day centre. This project was ultimately shelved due to costs. However Sue Sharples, who was joined by Michele Plant, the then manager of the Health Care Centre battled on relentlessly. The latter liaised with the Primary Care Trust (NHS) to get the day centre project off the ground. The Prison Service and the Governor had to be convinced that a separate building would be beneficial for those with a range of disabilities.

After months of tough negotiations it was decided that such a place would benefit the old and disabled, and would be a much better option than to allow them to stagnate in a cold and comfortless cell with only four walls and a television set for company. The paper work was rubber stamped and the Leyhill day centre was finally opened in 2006.

The centre comprises of a large comfortable room, which has a small kitchen at one end, and a large patio outside the entrance. Within the centre various activities take place, while painting is a favourite past time and the masterpieces that already grace the walls testify to the hidden talents of the old and infirm. Some paintings are either sold to raise cash for charitable purposes, or are entered for national prison awards, such as the Koestler.

For those unable to participate in the Fit for Life project, there are several other pursuits available; the extensive allotment for example, designed and constructed by one of the day centre users. It is here that the soil is tilled and tended with loving care and a huge variety of fruit and vegetables are grown and harvested.

Day centre users have an assortment of choices; they can go for walks within the perimeters of the vast sports field, provided it is organised and pre-arranged. There is also a sheltered bowling green, where many class matches have been won and lost.

Somewhere in between these activities there is still time for a brew-up, and tea is served, weather permitting, on the ample-sized flag-stone patio. The patio is surrounded by a wooden fence and part-raised garden. Hanging baskets adorn the centre's walls, which gives off an aura of a completely calm and stress free atmosphere.

Two professional carers help in the day to day running of the centre and they too participate in the activities on offer. They also understand that a positive and structured routine can, and does stimulate the mind as well as the body. 'Far better than working in the prison work shops,' said one man. 'A good alternative to work, which many of us can't do anyway.' said another. A further prisoner added; 'The day centre is a Godsend, for without it I'd be lost.'

Links have been forged with Stuart Ware, (Restore Support Network, which is in partnership with Age (UK) in Portsmouth, who support older people in prison and on release into the community. He visits the day centre at Leyhill on a monthly basis. Outside visitors come in to give talks on travel, and presentations by other prisoners who are taking various Key Skill level examinations in communication tend to be very popular.

Leyhill Prison is not run on the 'holiday camp' style atmosphere, which from time to time, some national media groups depict when there is nothing better to fill column inches. Many of the day centre prisoners are serving life sentences and have spent many years inside. Leyhill is the last leg of that journey where the aged and disabled are assessed for resettlement into the wider community. Therefore, if people like Sue Sharples, Michele Plant and governor Bell are willing to try and test such a venture; that can only mean that even the most severely disabled have a significantly brighter future to look forward to.

Perhaps this is not part of the history of Kingston prison, but in the long run it does have a knock-on effect for the majority of elderly prisoners will probably be transferred from Kingston to open prisons like Leyhill.

Punishment by Death

Although there is no longer capital punishment the following extract from Prison Service Manual may be worth noting. However Kingston Prison was not a hanging Prison, for all men that committed such heinous crimes were sent to Winchester. Yet it is still interesting to read and digest the following text concerning executions.

Capital punishment is retained in 92 countries and territories, including the USA (37 States), China, and Islamic countries. It was abolished in the United Kingdom in 1965 for all crimes except treason - but since the United Kingdom has joined the European Union, the death penalty has been abolished completely.

The last executions took place on August 13th, 1964, when Gwynne Evans, aged 24, and Peter Allen, aged 21, were hanged for the murder of John West, a laundry van driver, at Seaton in Cumbria. The pair died simultaneously in Manchester Strangeways prison and in Walton prison, Liverpool.

Statutory Rules for Prisoners under Sentence of Death.

The Governor will see that the scaffold and all the necessary appliances are in good order. The following articles, of which a stock is kept at Pentonville Prison, are necessary for an execution, and an early requisition for them will be forwarded to the Governor of that prison.

The rope.

The pinioning apparatus.

The cap.

A bag capable of containing sand to the same weight as the prisoner in clothes. This bag will be of the approved pattern, with a very thick neck, well padded on the outside with soft canvas to prevent any damage to the rope. No unnecessary experiments should be carried out either with the rope or bag.

A piece of chalk.

A few feet of copper wire.

A rule, or graduated pole, sixe feet long.

A piece of pack thread. (This should be just strong enough to support the rope without breaking).

A tackle to raise the bag of sand, or body, out of the pit.

Chain, including a shackle and pin.

A week before the execution, the rope will be thoroughly tested by a competent officer in accordance with directions, so that in case of any defect, a new one may be obtained.

On his arrival at the prison the day before the execution, the executioner will be furnished by the Governor and Medical Officer with all the necessary information as to the height and weight of the prisoner, his general condition, age, and whether he is likely to offer any resistance. The executioner should calculate the length of the drop required in each case (according to the 'table of drops' if adopted). The Governor and Medical Officer may recommend a departure from the table if, after examination, it appears there are special reasons for such a departure.

The Governor is authorised to pay, to each assistant executioner whom he may engage, and who is actually present at the execution, the sum of £3. 3 shillings, to cover all charges for each attendance, to allow reasonable travelling expenses—a warrant for a return 3rd class ticket at the cheapest possible rate, and such cab fares as shown to be absolutely necessary—and to provide lodging and maintenance while such persons are required to remain in the prison. He will see that each such person is properly lodged and boarded within the prison, that he receives all necessary assistance, and that he carries out his duty in due decorum.

The Governor will not allow casts to be taken of the heads of criminals who have been executed.

The authorities of the prison where the execution takes place will carry out the burial of executed criminals. Graves will not be distinguished in any way by names, initials, or other marks.

Prisoners under sentence of death will be placed generally on ordinary hospital diet with an addition, (e.g. egg and bacon for breakfast). The Medical Officer will see that no waste occurs.... Half a pint of beer may be allowed to a condemned prisoner at dinner, and again at supper, at the discretion of the medical officer.

Short Stories by Prisoners at Kingston.

Cockaleekie and Carrots.

Fred Logan pulled the hood of his anorak tighter over his ears and bent his body into the gusting snow storm, as he made his way to Edinburgh Waverley Station.

His mind was on the journey that lay ahead, and his thoughts periodically wandered to his family, who had only said their goodbyes to him a few hours before. Fred didn't want to go back, for he'd enjoyed the five days pre-Christmas home leave from the Scrubs - which had gone down well with a few beers and a couple of joints.

He checked his wrist watch and broke into a run, two minutes was all he had left to catch the Edinburgh to London express.

'Platform fifteen,' he mumbled to a uniformed guard.

'That way, Sir,' the guard replied, pointing in the direction of the all-night cafeteria.

Fred murmured a quick 'Merry Christmas,' and felt his legs carry him in that general direction. He could just make out platform fifteen, gate closed, train gathering speed down the Waverley incline. He was too late, for all he saw was a red taillight blinking in the cold darkness.

Fred punched a fist into his open palm, cursed under his breath and turned his six-foot frame sharply on his heels. There was nothing he could do now, except wait until the morning train, which was scheduled to run at twenty past six. He knew he would have to kill some time, and suddenly he remembered about an all-night bar at the back end of Princes' Street.

At least he'd be warm there, he thought, where the whisky came straight from the wood.

Fred made his way to the bar and slapped a twenty pound

note on the polished mahogany slab and called for the barman.

'Yes, Sir,' the barman said, smiling.

'A cockaleekie and carrots,' Fred drawled.

'A what!' the barman said with an astonished look on his face.

'You're new here, aren't you?' Fred said.

'Sure am, mate,' the barman replied. 'But tell me. What is a cockaleekie and carrots?'

'Johnny Walker, a twist of peel, and a large brandy tossed on top.

'Lemon or orange?' the barman grinned.

'Huh?'

'The peel... lemon or orange?'

'A cockaleekie and carrots always has orange,' Fred said, grabbing a high chrome stool and sitting firmly on its red-velvet top.

Whilst the drink was being mixed, Fred took time to take in his surroundings. A couple of timid looking characters sat in box-like alcoves brooding over pints of tartan - probably scared to death of their hatchet-faced wives, Fred thought, waiting for the beer to take effect before plucking up enough guts to face them.

Out of the corner of his eye, Fred saw this blonde haired girl step from the ladies' room and breeze up to the bar. She was a beautiful looking creature, Fred thought, with her long hair falling in a million tresses right past her slim shoulders. He gasped for air as she sat on the stool next to him.

'Merry Christmas, Darling,' she pouted. 'Will you buy me a drink?'

Fred's lungs gulped at the air. He slapped his hand on the shiny slab, yelling himself hoarse for the barman.

'One minute, Sir,' the barman shouted. 'I'll be there in a tick.'

No sooner had the barman placed Fred's cockaleekie and carrots in front of him, he was filling up a glass with ice and expertly pouring three fingers of the house's best scotch over the top.

'What's your name?' the girl asked Fred. She spoke with a slight country burr, which seemed to tickle at her throat.

'Fred... Fred Logan at your service.'

'I'm Sonia,' the girl purred softly.

'Are you married, Sonia?'

'Not any more,' she sighed. 'But I was married...' Sonia began to count her slim fingers. 'Six times, Darling. I've been down the aisle so many times, I've clean forgot the exact number.'

Fred pursed his lips and took out a packet of Benson and Hedges. He offered one to the girl and lit a match.

'No thanks,' Sonia said, shaking her head. 'That's one vice I don't believe in.'

Fred shrugged his shoulders. 'Do you mind if I have one?'

'Help yourself,' Sonia said. 'But I think it interferes with a man's performance.' She winked at Fred and fluttered her eyelashes.

Fred looked at the packet of Bensons, then at the box of matches, looked at Sonia again, and lit another match. Damn it! He thought, he needed a smoke - performance, good or bad.

'Do you live around here?' Fred asked, blowing out the match and dumping the charcoaled remains into an ashtray.

'Charlotte Square,' Sonia responded.

'Do you live on your own?'

'Sure...' Sonia swilled the ice around the bowl of her empty glass and flicked a wayward strand of hair from her eyes in the next movement.

'Bar!' Fred yelled.

'Sir.'

'We'll have the same again,' Fred said, squashing his half finished cigarette into the ashtray.

Sonia crossed her legs, and as she did so, her skirt rode high above her knees.

If this was a preview of what was to come, Fred thought, then he'd just go along with her and trust his luck.

They propped up the bar for several hours and Fred could see that Sonia was beginning to feel the pace of the drinking session.

'Shall I call a cab?' Fred volunteered. He took hold of Sonia's hand and felt the softness of her flesh against his.

At that moment the phone rang from somewhere behind the bar.

The barman plucked the contraption from its cradle and spoke into the mouthpiece.

'Sonia, who?' he muttered, turning towards Fred and the girl. 'Is your name, Sonia?'

'Yes,' Sonia whispered. She put her finger to her lips and beckoned the barman to her.

'Yes,' the barman said in a low tone.

'If it's Harry,' Sonia pouted. 'Tell him I've taken a hike to Gretna Green.'

The barman smiled, spoke swiftly into the mouthpiece and replaced the phone in its cradle.

'One of your... eh! Husbands?' Fred asked, rubbing his chin with a free hand.

'No,' Sonia said. 'It's this jerk who keeps on asking me to marry him.' She pulled a face and pursed her soft red lips.

'That bad?' Fred frowned.

Sonia nodded her head, swung herself from the high stool and planted a warm kiss right on Fred's willing mouth.

'I'll be back in a minute,' Sonia whispered over her shoulder, then made her way to the ladies' room.

Whilst Sonia was making up her face, Fred took the opportunity to adjust his anorak zip and run nervous fingers through his hair. He winked at his reflection in the mirror and mumbled a few greasy words about the chaps in the Scrubs. He couldn't wait to get back to tell them all about Sonia, for it wasn't every Christmas a fellah came across such a good looking girl, he thought.

It was only a ten minute cab ride to Sonia's place. Fred tipped the cabby a fiver, for that's how pleased he was at his blessed luck.

It was a basement flat where Sonia had her rooms, and it was a neat place that she had. Everything was just where it should be in a girl's apartment. Fred glanced through into the bedroom - a soft looking eiderdown covered a king-sized bed, and musky perfume drifted to his nostrils.

Sonia fell on to the three seater, skirt riding high on her thighs.

'I'll take a shower, Honey,' Fred gulped.

'Sure,' Sonia responded. 'I'll be in the bedroom when you've finished.'

Fred took his leave, undressed, and began to shower, gently closing the cubicle's door behind him. He carefully soaped his six-foot frame as the hot spray pummelled his back, and he must have been in there the best part of an hour.

When he'd finished he made his way to the bedroom.

Gingerly, he pushed the door open.

The lights were out.

'Sonia?' he whispered. 'Sonia?'

There was no reply, so he fumbled for the light switch, found it, and flicked it on. He was absolutely shocked by what he saw. Sonia was there all right - but naked as the day she was born - well, almost. A black silk stocking was all she wore, and that was tied tightly around her pretty neck... on all accounts, Sonia was dead.

'Christ!' Fred muttered. 'I'll have to get the hell out of here.'

It took what seemed like hours for him to dress himself. He then grabbed a duster and polished everything he could remember that he'd touched.

Then the door bell rang like crazy. Sweat poured down Fred's ashen face. He froze for a moment, ran into the back kitchen and stared ominously at the barred window - no escape here, he thought.

When he did manage to re-enter the lounge, the place was simply buzzing with cops. Four of them had his arms cuffed firmly behind his back, and before he could wish them all a Merry Christmas, he was taken to the local police station and charged accordingly.

'Have you anything to say?' the desk sergeant asked.

By that time Fred was completely incoherent, but managed to mumble a few words.

'What's that?' the desk sergeant spat. 'C'mon, man. Speak up!'

'I said. I wish I hadn't drunk so many cockaleekie's and carrots.'

The Satanic Salesman

I could see Kennedy airport, lights twinkling like firefly's, aircraft taking off and landing, busy chequered cabs speeding towards the tall buildings of the bustling metropolis known as the big apple.

As the airport came nearer, I could hear the thunderous roar of Pratt and Whitney engines and make out the clouds of chilly vapour that clung around the parked jets. It was November - misty and battleship grey as a man o' war - the sullen red sun was already sinking behind the far hills.

The smell of aircraft fuel made me feel like throwing up, so I wound up the window and took my lane, sliding the Hertz rental towards the slab of hard concrete, which was the car park.

My flight wasn't until twenty after nine, I'd kill some time in the airport lounge - maybe have a few Jack Daniels', maybe even some beer.

I sat down in a luxurious chair and called the waiter, gave him my order and smiled.

'Ice, Sir?' he said in a high pitched voice.

'Yeah,' I drawled. He reminded me of some faggot that tried to get over familiar with me, on one of my frequent binges down Madison and Fifth. I watched as he walked to the bar, hips swinging like a broad from Harlem; I had to laugh.

The waiter returned clutching a round tray above his head my Jack Daniels, precariously perched on top was festooned in plastic flowers and palm trees, and smelt like the botanic gardens. He smiled sweetly and placed the drink on the table in front of me.

'Sir,' he said. 'The lady over at the bar has picked up the bill.'

I glanced towards the upholstered bar and saw this broad sitting on a high chrome stool, the shiny metal matched her hair perfectly; the red velvet elbow-rest complimented her full lips.

Whistling softly, gently easing myself from the comfortable chair, I sauntered over. Her wine red lips parted into a smile, tongue teasingly licking the soft flesh, the blue eyes flashing.

'Hey, Honey,' she said. 'I'm Sareeta and I'm flying down on old red eye tonight.'

'Jeez,' I slapped my thigh and pulled up a scaffold beside her. 'Me too, Honey,' I grinned.

'What do I call you?' she whispered in a southern drawl.

'Nick,' I responded, 'Nick Devlin at your service.'

'Are you working down in Frisco?'

'Yeah,' I said. 'I'm a travelling salesman.'

'Brushes?' She looked bewildered.

I laughed when she said that, Brushes indeed.

'Well? ' She queried, looking at me with those big blue eyes.

'What do you sell?'

'Top secret, I told her.

She swivelled glumly in her chair and raised the glass; 'Here's looking at you, Honey,' she said seductively.

We propped up the bar for several hours and I was amazed at how quickly time had passed. The lounge, where all the red eye passengers gathered - had no more than twenty souls. I checked my timepiece with the clock on the wall and threw back the last Jack Daniels' and winked at Sareeta. I heard the pleasant voice of the announcer, requesting the passengers for flight 666, to make their way to gate nine.

'Well what do you know,' laughed Sareeta. 'We're on the Devil's flight tonight.'

'Hell;' I muttered. So this was why the lounge was so empty - brushes indeed.

I forced my six foot frame out of the chrome scaffold and looked in the mirror, slicked back my raven coloured hair and ran a wet finger across my dark bushy brows. Well - okay, so I was vain,

Sareeta powdered her nose right there in the lounge, the paint brushes came out and with deft strokes the red lips were touched up - like, well, like Whistler painting a masterpiece - no wonder they called this flight the red eye, and I was looking forward to it very much. The journey from New York to San Francisco would take at least five hours of night time flying - easily the longest anywhere in the USA. To me, this was a prestige job and I was thrilled at the prospects that would eventually come my way - a big change from my usual patch in Maine.

The announcer's voice rang through the P.A. system requesting again that we should, hurry to gate nine. I don't remember whether Sareeta held me up, or vice versa - but anyway, together, we safely boarded the D.C.9. There wasn't much to see from thirty thousand feet above the dark blanket of clouds, but Sareeta insisted on sitting by the window.

'You never know,' she said in all seriousness. 'I just might see a flying saucer.'

'Sure, Honey,' I shrugged. 'You never can tell.'

Me, well I was quite content in guzzling my Jack Daniels and carefully studying the other passengers. Fifteen I counted, including Sareeta and myself. Five had obviously changed their minds and waited for the morning flight - but I wasn't worried; I was only a salesman and like I said, this was a prestige job, and if the airline wanted to lose money, then that was the airline's problem. I was quite happy what my boss paid me and promotion was far better than earthly possessions.

I glanced at Sareeta from time to time whilst her own eyes took in the starlit night, and wondered, what can this broad do, a dancer, I guessed. But certainly not the movie starlet she made out to be.

The other passengers were a mixed bunch; a couple on their way to be married, four loud businessmen - who were making jokes about the flight number. The remaining seven were just ordinary everyday folks and, of course, there was the air-crew - twenty four all told. This D.C.9 was certainly running at a loss, bad salesmanship? Or plain superstition, I could probably guess correctly...

Sareeta's nudge in the ribs brought me back to reality.

'Yeah? ' I said, following her pointing finger. 'What's the

matter?'

'What do you think that is?' she whispered.

Her face took on a deathly pallor as I leaned over her trim form and gazed out the window.

'Thunder storm,' I said simply. 'But don't worry it's a long way off.'

'I'm scared,' she said. 'Could I.... Could I change seats?'

'Sure,' I responded. 'But it's a ...'

Before I could finish she was up and waiting for me to move seats. I had no choice but to obey her whim.

Sitting down in my seat, she immediately strapped herself in and pulled her neck into her shoulders.

I couldn't help but laugh, and when I laugh it comes straight from the belly. The other passengers turned and stared - wondering, wondering what the hell was going on.

I never stopped laughing not even when the lightning bolt struck the tail of the aircraft and sent it spinning towards the rocky terra firma. But I heard the screams of panic, saw the contorted faces of the passengers as they were thrown about like cabbage patch dolls - how could anyone survive.

I was first through the gates of hell airport, the rest of the passengers and the air-crew, reluctantly followed, the loud businessmen, somewhat quiet. I didn't have to guess what was running through their minds, I already knew.

They were all taken to the airport transit hotel, where they would stay for a short period of time - and after some slight adjustments they would soon get over the traumatic experience. Of course, some would take longer... like Sareeta.

It was two weeks later when I next saw her, she was still at the hotel, alone, and wretchedly uncomfortable. She smiled faintly when I entered her dark and dreary room, windowless, and without mirrors. I took a step backwards, but then paused, and looked at her again.

'Nick,' she pleaded. 'Only you can help me get away from here.'

'I can't,' I told her. 'You must stay here now.'

She was silent for a moment - then she said, 'Perhaps I'm

frightened over nothing at all. Perhaps it's something neither heaven nor earth knows anything about.'

'And what does that leave you,' I whispered.

'That only leaves hell,' she screamed. 'But can't you see I'm alive.... Alive and kicking.'

'Sure, Honey,' I shrugged. 'If you say so.' I tossed her the hand bag she kept the paint brushes in, 'Here, make yourself pretty, for my boss wants to see you.'

She took the bag and, in true movie star fashion, composed herself and took out the powder compact. Flicking back the lid, she stared into the mirror and then it hit her like a boxing glove - for there was no reflection.

Any director would have been proud of the performance that she put on - the screams were first class, worthy even of an encore.

I can still hear her screams, even now as I sit here at O'Hare airport a large Jack Daniels in one hand and a broad in the other. Of course, I was promoted after the red eye flight and put in charge of the Chicago end of the business - and O'Hare was simply buzzing with 747's filled to capacity - brushes indeed.

Poems by Prisoners

The Last Fence

Skewbald and frisky and patched like a cow
Flash little jumper and can't half row.
A bit dodgy in traffic, can't understand why
But can rein in tight at the cast of a die.
He's not all that pushy, but he'll try his darned best
I wish he'd grow up and be like the rest.
With quiet resignation he stands in his stall,
Awaiting the grass to grow lush, green, and tall.
But when he's out in the morning with me
He gallops and kicks for that hour when he's free.
Much like a woman, he has a sort of sixth sense
One final first place when he jumps that last fence.

My Broken Radio

My broken radio was a complete eyesore
So to the vicar, I did implore.
Could you get me, a new one my old son?
For the broken one cost me over a ton.
Look here, young man, he said to me
Call back and see me after tea.
So off I went, with a cheery smile
Down to 'A' wing about a mile.
Later on I came straight back
The vicar looked way off track.
I'm in the business of saving souls
Not mending radio's full of holes.
With that, I took it, my luck was out
So that's what volumetric control was about.

Note; Volumetric control is a means of keeping tags on a prisoner's
property; i.e. two equal size boxes filled to the brim and no more.

Photo - Fit

He seemed an honest chap
Smartly dressed
Trilby hat
Oval face
And more than that
He seemed an honest chap.
Mobile phone
Plastic cash
Wide smile
And more than that
He seemed an honest chap.
Shiny shoes
No crap
Black gloves
And more than that
He seemed an honest chap.
Strong grip
Warm heart
Never sick
And more than that
He seemed an honest chap.
Photo – fit
Didn't scrap
Answered to Mick
And more than that
He seemed an honest chap.
London Bridge
St James's Park
Sold the lot
And more than that
He seemed an honest chap.

Riding White Horses

Come ride the white horse
The horse dealer cried
You'll have a great trip
He usually lied.

The first rides for free
Those words did the trick
I rode off on her back
But after felt sick.

The next time I saw him
I asked after his horse
I wanted to ride
He said, but of course.

He charged me ten dollars
This seemed kind of mean
I rode to a heaven,
Where I'd never been.

When the journey was over
The horse brought me back
To a new hell on earth,
Where I need more smack.

I sought the horse dealer
And begged him for more
My pride and ten dollars
It cost me to score.

The horse ran from heaven
To hell with my soul
I'm no longer the master
The horse had control.

The dealer looked different
Horns, hoofs and tail
Upon my return
A guaranteed sale.

Fixed up once more
To the heavens I rode
I tried chasing dragons
It cost me much gold.

White horses cost plenty
And my money had gone
So I stole for the habit
Though I knew it was wrong.

In prison, white horses
Are not allowed in
I shivered, grew sick
And my body turned thin.

That is my story
Of my horse riding days
Now I'm left with nothing
But the memories don't haze

So I ride the white horse
But ride it well
For the white horse of heroin
Will take you to hell.

The writer of this poem was later transferred out of Kingston to another prison, for a prisoner died of a drug overdose and the former was held whilst an investigation was carried out. Two years later the poet was exonerated and put on normal location at Maidstone.

I Am Me

I am who I am and there is no one else quite like me. All my fellow beings are similar, but none of them resemble, or act like me, even my DNA structure confirms that I am different from everyone else. Moreover, the sweat that drips from my skin after a strenuous workout belongs to me, as does the emotional tears of sadness or happiness, which run freely down my cheeks.

My thoughts, dreams, fantasies and feelings are private matters, as are my ideas and all I see with my eyes. What's more I know that some irregularities have to be controlled in such a way so as not to offend others. The words I speak are my property, whether my voice is soft, harsh or loud. Therefore, whatever actions I respond to are of my own volition and I take the consequences of those actions, which only I am answerable.

My trials and tribulations are down to me and nobody else. I decide who and what I love and what I don't love. There by it's my choice to bring an end to anything I don't want to pursue – in my own good time.

Of course there are certain things I don't like about myself, which cause puzzlement, but as long as I have the confidence I can ponder over anything that bewilders me and try and solve any problems to the best of my ability. I can stand back and take a good look at myself, go over the points I've said or done, and check out how I felt at that given moment in time – only then can I safely deal with any issues that crop up.

Some parts might be unfitting, but I can get rid of anything that proves to be inappropriate, hold on to what's suitable and attempt to invent something new to replace what I discard. I realise more than anyone else that I can see, feel, hear, think, and try to make sense in what I do; for I have been given the tools in which to survive. I make the decisions as to how I use those tools to become a better person; for I am the sole engineer of my own destiny.

However, I'm not completely stupid or arrogant, for I also know that I need help on the way and it is my responsibility to take up any offers of support from friends and trusted advisors. In the main some people may not find that I'm agreeable, and well past my sell-by-date, but if they take time out and get to know me, they'll find out that I am Me, and I am okay!

An Interview With Trevor Payne

Trevor Payne, Head of education at Kingston prison retired in April 1999 and here follows an interview by the editor of Kingston Magazine; K.M.

Trevor Payne will have retired to the sun-kissed beaches at Southsea with his bucket and spade before anyone has finished reading issue two of KM. However I managed to track him down before his train pulled out of Fratton station.

It was on one of Fratton's damp and windswept platforms where Trevor told me that he was married with three children and has four grandchildren. He also told me that he had two very interesting careers.

It is not generally known that Trevor has been employed in prisons for many years. I asked him a little about his first career.

I am a Methodist minister and worked in London (Regent Street Polytechnic), Norfolk, Leicester, and Gloucester. After nineteen years in local church work, which included various chaplaincies, then the RAF, University and prison? I was given permission by the church to work full-time in prison education, providing someone gave me a job. Since then I worked in Eastwood Park DC for a year and six years in Gloucester prison before coming to Kingston in 1985.

My ears were burning with interest as I scribbled down his next words. I was amazed that such a nice level-headed person could cause a near riot situation in a prison – any prison. However, by the time Trevor finished what he was saying I soon found out differently.

'I remember,' he said in soft tones. 'When I caused a crisis in Pentonville and got locked up in the chapel alone. I thought to ring the bell more than once would make it sound like an emergency. So I rang it once and the 'A' Team piled in. 'Was my face red?'

I smiled when he said that.... Could you imagine, our Trevor, red-faced and looking piously at the ceiling murmuring a prayer to the Lord when the 'A' Team burst in?

After gathering my composure I managed to rattle off the next question. He went on to tell me that he did a lot of teaching in the church and both careers fitted in well together.

'I feel,' he said. 'That education In prison as a preparation for release and help to remain a real person inside.'

Trevor's Bristol accent was still detectable as he explained that dealing with a situation when a teacher was suspected of wrong-doing, was the most difficult situation he had encountered in a prison.

'I've never experienced the slightest difficulty with attitudes or behaviour of prisoners. He said in conclusion.

I nodded my head as this yoga loving man told me that he would not have chosen any other career, apart from the ones he had already had. I took this opportunity to ask about his time at Kingston.

'Some may remember Annette Jordan' He recalled. 'Annette and I were approached with a brief to build up the education programme at Kingston and were given the resources to do this over several years. I've always tried to make the programme reflect the actual needs of those who were here at any given time.'

The words; 'The actual needs of those who were here at any given time.' Made me think about the assertiveness and decision making course organised by Trevor in conjunction with the education department and Highbury College.

'It is not always recognised that aggressive people can benefit from assertiveness change as much as passive people.' He said. 'We all need the negotiating skills and the understanding of other people's point of view.'

To save a long drawn-out argument I compromised and agreed not to disagree with him. Trevor glanced at his wristwatch as I turned yet another page. I asked him his views concerning innocent men who languished in prison – even Kingston.

'It is very difficult' he said. 'To make a judgement without the full facts, but in a few cases I have felt that a real injustice has been done.'

The train was beginning to pull out of Fratton station; the guard blew hard on his whistle. I needed more time, for there were so many questions I wanted to ask.

I could have sworn I heard Mozart's piano concerto fill the air. This was followed by wonderful orchestral music by Prokofiev; both of which are Trevor's favourite composers. As the train picked up speed I waved him off.

When it disappeared from view I wondered if Trevor was looking forward to his retirement. No doubt he was, I thought, but would he take some time out to pay a return visit to Kingston.

If it were not for him enjoying the high life on those sun-kissed beaches at Southsea, he probably would, I guessed.

Don't say goodbye – say Sayonara.

Can we forget you?
Even for the time it takes
A flash of lightning
To shine across
The autumn fields of corn.

None of my Best Friends are Murderers

This article has been produced in response to Jonathan Bradley's well-written piece concerning Writers' in Residence in Prison. (Writers' Forum, Volume 5, Issue 3). The article's intent is to give readers some inside information into the pitfalls of a Resident Writer in Prison, as opposed to a Writer in Residence in Prison.

I'd like to be straight up-front and tell you that it took a well-aimed squirt of machine oil into the bowels of my old Imperial typewriter before this piece was polished up enough for final submission.

In the meantime I'd like to say that none of my best friends are murderers, and that I'm not duty-bound by the Official Secrets Act.

However, as a convicted prisoner, I could probably think of a few scarier six-word phrases than the comparatively tame; 'Freeze, and hand over your wallet.' Or; 'Have you considered taking early retirement.'

Sometimes, as a writer, and a prisoner, it makes me wonder if the public believe that most, if not all gangsters are proper gentlemen. Take my word for it, gangsters and muggers would rip your head off if they thought there was an unclaimed lottery ticket stitched up in the lining of your wallet. They certainly wouldn't give a toss if you were saving up for early retirement. Or for that matter, if you were a dodgy character waiting to be crushed up into a Sardine tin in an East London car breaker's yard.

I'm not having a go at you, Jonathan. But some of those prisoners you teach should have come up with far more realistic phrases than the ones you presented us with - or does that breach the Official Secrets Act!

I've been inside for a bit longer than Jonathan's two-year stretch as a Writer in Residence in Prison, and the only interviews I had were with the Regional Crime Squad and an Old Bailey Judge.

As a writer, however, my struggle continues, and I've tried my best as the years have slipped into oblivion. I feel that I am still serving out my apprenticeship and learning new tricks every day from many different angles and viewpoints. Above all I've learnt to take criticism, and I no longer fly into a rage when a rejection slip is shoved through my letter box.

When I first decided to take up writing, I had to submit a short story to the writing school as a sort of taster. My self esteem rocketed through the roof when I read their letter of acceptance into the wonderful world of writers. My piece, they said, was 'evocative,' and that writing was in my veins. So I enrolled and posted off the cheque.

Writing was a bit of a struggle in the beginning and I was lucky to complete the two-year course in half the time. A few months after finishing the writers' course I was transferred to another prison. Again my luck held, for they had a qualified writing tutor in that establishment - writers' in residence, and Jonathan had yet to arrive in the penal system.

Jonathan reflected that he had to produce something. For example, a structured anthology of prisoners' work, a radio play, or a prison magazine, and maybe even bring in a few poets and authors to beef up the workshop readings.

I hope Jonathan was more successful than I in securing the expertise of eminent poets and authors. I had Jeffrey Archer lined up to give a lecture on the art of creative writing - but that fell through and again I was on the move.

Perhaps Jonathan was right when he said that some members of staff in prisons don't like Arts Workers, and that prisoners don't deserve such luxuries. Maybe prison staff thought it was as if I was one of those Arty radical subversives mentioned by Jonathan in his article.

Writing, especially in prison does me the power of good. It builds up my self esteem, keeps me sane, and if I'm lucky I can earn myself a few shekels on the side. Most of all it helps in rehabilitating me, and this without the interference from the

Prison Officers Association - or breaching the Official Secrets Act.

A few years ago I had one of my long manuscripts appraised. I was quite shocked when I was told that my mood changes showed up in the text. On checking over the manuscript I realized that what I was told was true, and where the text became slapdash, coincided with my moves from prison to prison. So in that sense I am no different from writers in the free world; and I yearn for the freedom of choice to beaver away in a relaxed and stable atmosphere.

I have no problem writing once I get the first paragraph down on a sheet of A4 paper, and I'm pretty strict when it comes to self-discipline. For without self-discipline I would be afraid that my mood swings would crop up again in my writing.

Staying with the subject of manuscripts I can never understand the mentality of some prison Governors when they tell me that I'm not allowed to send pieces to publishers. These officials jab their finger at me and are careful to point out, that as a convicted prisoner, I'm not allowed to run a business from prison. However, I hastily add that it's not me who is running the business, and that I'm only offering a commodity.

Believe me when I tell you that I do my utmost to side-step negative thinking people like this. For I try to avoid flat characters as I would avoid a rabid dog doing its best to get friendly with me in the local municipal peace gardens.

I set my scenes with interesting characters and put them in situations of conflict, and then as the plot unfolds I explore how these characters resolve the conflict. A bit similar to setting up a job and knowing where the police are going to be when one of Jonathan's pupils forgets where he stashed the keys to the getaway car.

That reminds me why I've spent many a rotten hour banged up tight in my cell, scratching my head and nibbling away at the end of my pencil - wondering why the plots have stopped appearing. When that little gem of a plot eventually hits me like a boxing glove I sometimes forget the rule about using too many clichés as I sit down and get stuck into the nuts and bolts of creative writing. In the meantime I wish Jonathan all the best in his post, and I'm looking forward to reading the remaining part of his interesting article.

Kingston Prison did have a Writer in Residence and he was a wonderful chap.

End Game

As a convicted prisoner I've had the misfortune to have been on the dizzy merry-go-round of prisons. I've walked the landings of numerous prisons and witnessed terrible deeds that prisoners have inflicted on their fellow human beings; nasty, inhumane crimes that even the International Court at The Hague would frown upon.

I've made the cardboard furniture in the 'Scrubs', which was then used in segregation units in prisons up and down the country.

I've survived the battles and prison politics that are an every day occurrence within the prison system. At the beginning I made a conscious decision that the only way to survive in prison – was to fight back.

Many adjudications, and outside court appearances meant that my original tariff of seven years was extended to almost twenty three years.

However, in the year 2013 and beyond the onus will be on protecting the public, which is more important than releasing prisoners on parole. Oh yes, the prisons are full to bursting point – no lessons learnt after the prison riot at Strangeways, but the Government and the new Ministry of Justice is adamant that those sent to prison for serious crimes will, and must be kept inside for as long as is necessary to appease and ensure the public is protected.

Of course new sentencing policies will be introduced; some have already been implemented and they include; electronic tagging, Anti Social Behaviour Orders, more stringent community work, and tiring and irksome labour. If these men and women still won't conform to the system, or disobey the law, then they will go straight to prison. Some life sentences will be abolished and replaced by a prison term.

Government at one time considered the implementation of austere conditions within the penal system - but this was frowned on by some as being a political ploy in the search for votes. However, many years ago, conditions in the penal system were far worse than they are today.

Take the proclamation of the Rev. Sidney Smith, when he said that 'Prison should be a terror to evil doers,' He went on to say; 'There must be no visiting of friends, no education but religious education, no weavers' looms or carpenters' benches. There must be a great deal of solitude; coarse food; a dress of shame; hard, incessant, irksome eternal labour a planned and regulated and unrelenting exclusion of happiness and comfort.'

Of course, in this day and age even the public would frown on such drastic measures. But the Prison Service runs in tandem with the Probation Service and the Ministry of Justice. New and bold steps have been implemented concerning the after care of prisoners about to be released, dangerous or otherwise.

An OASYS is conducted, which is scored to various degrees and levels of dangerousness. Then a MAPPA Board sits and a decision is made as to what level of risk the prisoner could pose, and these are; Level one, low risk, which can be managed by one probation officer. Level two, medium risk, which can be managed by a probation officer and the police. Level three, which can be managed by a probation officer, the police and a psychologist and perhaps even one other agency. This is all for the benefit of protecting the public, and to ensure the released prisoner abides by the rules laid down by the MAPPA Board.

Believe it or not prisons are getting better all the time and some establishments even allow laptop computers in-cell, but without the internet connection. DVD players, printers, digital boxes, table lamps, and many other so-called 'home comforts.'

Then what about the future, say in one hundred years time, what will prisons be like then? Who will run them? How many men and women will be incarcerated in penal establishments on this small, but overcrowded Island. (There is over 85,000 men and women in prison and this will rise if the government decides to build huge 2,500 place Titan prisons; for by 2014 there could be around 96,000 prisoners locked up).

Right now I'm willing to make a prediction that there will be no prisons as we know them and no prison officers. Huge prison colonies run by robots? Smacks a bit like transportation to Australia and the like.

What about the moon? Nah, that's a bit far fetched. Okay, then what about giant space colonies in constant orbit around the earth.

Imagine massive spaceships that can accommodate thousands of prisoners; men and women locked up in prison space ships awaiting further transportation beyond the stars to colonise far flung planets.

What about the return of the death penalty for even the most trivial of offences. Something akin to the 17th and 18th century way of thinking; the crash of the trapdoor as a felon is hurled into oblivion – his crime, that of stealing a pig or a sheep.

No, it will not quite come to that, but in one hundred years time, no doubt someone will come up with some form of execution the general public will be able to digest and swallow more easily. Perhaps even death by euphoria, which could be a pleasant way to die and that will be the end game as far as criminals are concerned.

However, these are only speculative thoughts and ideas – nothing to do with reality, but can anyone be absolutely certain that Kingston prison could, or could not be used as a holding centre for dangerous prisoners awaiting transportation to space colonies.... food for thought?

Sandy Malone.

Kingston Prison, 2013.

Deaths in Kingston; 1999.

There were many deaths in Kingston , especially from 'Death Row.' This was where the very old (many in their eighties) who were still considered too dangerous to be released.

However there was one particular lifer at Kingston known as 'Black Bob,' an Indian of Canadian nationality who was struck down by a severe bout of influenza as were many other prisoners. This story is told through the eyes of another prisoner.

'I befriended 'Bob' soon after he arrived from HMP Wormwood scrubs in London. He was around fifty years old and sported a bushy black beard and he tended to sway from one foot to the other when he spoke to anyone.

However as I was going down 'A' wing stairs to report sick I noticed that Bob was sprawled out writhing on the top of his bed. I went in and asked how he was and he asked if I could get a medic for him. He looked in a really ad way and off I went.

Bob's cell was at the foot of the stairs on 'A' wing and about four cells away from the office. I went into the office and explained to officer Dave Alum that Bob needs immediate attention and the Sick Bay staff do not arrive until nine. Dave Alum immediately phoned the main gate for an emergency ambulance and one arrived shortly after from St Mary's Hospital nearby to take Bob away. Sadly though, it was too late, for Bob died on the way.

Two weeks later Bob's relatives travelled from Canada for a special church service to commemorate his life. The service was well attended for Bob was a very likable prisoner.

A Prisoner commits suicide.

One morning the prison was opened up as usual, but were told not to go for breakfast for a prisoner had hung himself sometime during the night.

The deceased man was found when the morning staff came on duty (officers have to take a roll check prior to opening up) It was then that this tragedy was discovered. What was unusual was that the Governor (Stuart McClean) allowed the prisoners to mingle on 'A' wing landing, which overlooked the annex.

One prisoner who was very religious asked the Governor if it was all right to enter the deceased man's cell and say a prayer for him.

The Governor said no because the deceased was in fact a Muslim.

A few Tit Bits From Kingston Prison

It was no generally known that quite a few officers that worked at Kingston were ex Royal Navy. This was not surprising considering Portsmouth is a Naval Port..

It was not uncommon to see a prisoner walking round the football field talking to some ex shipmates that he served with on board various ships during his time at sea.

However, it was not at all uncommon for other prisoners in passing to sneer and whisper. 'Who are you grassing up now, mate?'

The prisoner walking with the officer curtly replied. 'No one, mate, I served on board the same ship as this officer and he is still an old shipmate of mine and there are several more screws here that I knew from my Navy days.'

No Prison Magazine?

When the prison was without a monthly magazine due to lack of funding a prisoner approached the governor and suggested that if he could raise the necessary cash, would he allow a prison magazine? The governor agreed.

This prisoner wrote many letters to local companies asking for cash or redundant computers. The prisoner was surprised when he received a computer from IBM and another from Radio South Coast.

A cheque for £100 was also sent by the novelist, Jeffrey Archer and the Kingston Prison magazine (KM) took off.

Officer Dick Vidler.

Officer Dick Vidler travelled from the Isle of Wight every day to work at Kingston Prison. Prior to working in Kingston he worked in Albany Prison. Dick Vidler was dissatisfied by the way certain prisoners at Albany were treated, so he transferred to Kingston.

Dick Vidler was ex RAF, a proper gentleman and a well-liked officer. Every Christmas Eve he dressed up as Santa Clause and at 2100 hours he personally locked up all the prisoners, wishing them a merry Christmas. A couple of old lags even left a few mince pies and a orange drink outside their cell door— appreciation for Santa, well yes, but more appreciation for Dick Vidler.

Lo and behold Dick Vidler added a further box of mince pies to the ones already outside those cell doors.

The Major Getting up Steam.

A prisoner who was well-known within the prison and known as 'The Major' used to take regular exercise around the football field. Suddenly, and without warning he would make a mad dash of about fifty yards.

One day an officer ordered a prisoner to stop 'The Major' from taking off and leaping over the wall, saying: 'If he takes off and manages to jump over the wall, I am ordering you to go and fetch him back'.

It transpired that 'The Major' was a train driver in the age of steam prior to his conviction. It was, however comical to watch this prisoner who was in his seventies regularly put on a fifty yard spurt as if he was getting up steam.

The Closure of Kingston Prison

Her Majesty's Prison Kingston fell foul of the Governments axe when it was closed on the 1st of April 2013. What will happen to the prison? Some members of the public want to keep it and used as a tourist attraction. Others would like to see another complex similar to Gunwharf, which the prison and the surrounding area would hold such a project. But most importantly Portsmouth must keep the structure intact. Think of the tourism possibilities? But remember, one can't change history and if it was demolished it would never be put back.

Prison tour booked out.

The chance to see inside a closed prison attracted a lot of interest. Recently closed HMP Kingston, on Milton Road, will be opening its gates on September 14 and 15 and tours are fully booked.

The opportunity will offer people the chance to see the Victorian wings or take a stroll round the exercise yards and see the workshops and kitchens.

The events are being run by the Ministry of Justice, which still owns the prison. The 'News' was told that no decision has been made over the prisons future.

Courtesy, Portsmouth News.

Keep Prison Tours Going.

One member of the public was very disappointed to find out that the tours of Kingston Prison were fully booked and was certain that lots of members of the public would show great interest in having a look around the prison. The writer in question would have liked the tour days extended, if only for the interest such an edifice would attract.

Crimes and sentences; 2013.

Here follows some of the crimes committed in Portsmouth and sentences meted out by the courts, but not serious enough to be incarcerated within Kingston Prison's sombre grey walls.

A woman from Havant admitted assault and was given a six month community order with a supervision requirement and must pay£85 costs plus a £60 victim surcharge.

A Portsmouth man admitted an assault and damaging a front door belonging to Portsmouth Council. He was given a six-month conditional discharge and must pay £160 compensation, a £10 fine and a £15 victim surcharge.

A Southsea man admitted stealing clothing worth £213 from Matalan in Portsmouth, using threatening and abusive behaviour and two counts of making off without paying for fuel worth a total of £128.17, in Southsea. He was given a two year conditional discharge and must pay £128.17 compensation plus a £15 victim surcharge.

A man from Waterlooville admitted driving without insurance, driving without a correct licence, driving while using a mobile phone and obstructing a police officer. He was fined £550 and must pay £85 costs plus £40 victim surcharge. He was banned from driving for 56 days.

A Portsmouth woman admitted four counts of stealing cash worth a total of £678. She was given a 12 week jail sentence, suspended for 12 months, and was also given a 12 month supervision requirement and must attend a woman's programme for 12 sessions. She must also £90 compensation and an £80 victim surcharge.

Courtesy Portsmouth News.

This is where it ends

To complete this Souvenir History of Kingston Prison I have inserted this highly emotionally charged poem by a lifer who served time at the prison and was HIV positive.

This is where it ends

Why am I lonely, Why am I sad
I know I've done wrong, but I'm not all that bad
I've made some mistakes, like we all do, I guess
But this time it's too late, now look at the mess.

I gambled my future by chasing a dream
And I'm left with my memories that aren't what they seem
The sun never shines and I cry for a while
For the virus I have makes it so hard to smile.

The stream where we laughed doesn't ripple; It's dry
And the songbirds have gone now, oh just let me die
My life is so empty, I can't stand the pain
And I don't think there's time to love someone again.

I'm frightened of darkness and dread every day
I have lost all direction and can't find my way
I long for some kindness, that's not asking much
Is there anyone out there to reach out and touch.

Just someone to talk to by giving and sharing
Believing in waiting, loving and caring
But my tears start again and I'm sad like before
So I will go now, I can't stand the pain anymore.

Hi, I'm here lads with the Christmas booty! Merry Christmas.

The above Christmas card was printed at Kingston Prison and many prisoners sent them out to family and friends. (Artist unknown).

The food at Kingston Prison wasn't as bad as this; but the cooks were working on it before the prison closed.

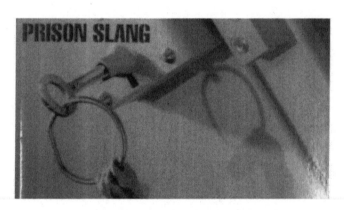

www.absonbooks.co.uk (Prison Slang; £1.99).

NOTES

NOTES

NOTES

NOTES

NOTES